Come Follow Me

Come Follow Me

Reflections on the Markan Jesus

S. H. Mathews

WIPF & STOCK · Eugene, Oregon

COME FOLLOW ME
Reflections on the Markan Jesus

Copyright © 2016 S. H. Mathews. All rights reserved. Except for brief quotations in critical publications or reviews, no part of this book may be reproduced in any manner without prior written permission from the publisher. Write: Permissions, Wipf and Stock Publishers, 199 W. 8th Ave., Suite 3, Eugene, OR 97401.

Wipf & Stock
An Imprint of Wipf and Stock Publishers
199 W. 8th Ave., Suite 3
Eugene, OR 97401

www.wipfandstock.com

PAPERBACK ISBN: 978-1-5326-0517-8
HARDCOVER ISBN: 978-1-5326-0519-2
EBOOK ISBN: 978-1-5326-0518-5

Manufactured in the U.S.A.　　　　　　　　　OCTOBER 25, 2016

Scripture quotations taken from the New International Version
Copyright © 1973, 1978, 1984 by International Bible Society

Dedicated to my fellow workers in the Kingdom of God at United Baptist Church in Valdese, North Carolina. This book is a product of your inquisitive minds, open hearts, and faithful lives. Thank you for inspiring me to walk straighter, to dig deeper, and to love more authentically.

Contents

Introduction | ix

1. Jesus Calls Us to Follow Him—Mark 1:16-20 | 1
2. Jesus Trades Places With us—Mark 1:40-45 | 5
3. Jesus Values the Soul Above the Body—Mark 2:1-12 | 8
4. Jesus Changes Everything—Mark 2:18-22 | 12
5. Why Was Jesus Angry?—Mark 3:1-6 | 16
6. Jesus Can Pardon All Sins But One—Mark 3:28-30 | 19
7. Cultivation of the Heart—Mark 4:13-20 | 22
8. Jesus Calms the Sea—Mark 4:35-41 | 25
9. Jesus Sends His First Missionary—Mark 5:18-20 | 28
10. Jesus Sends out the Twelve—Mark 6:7-13 | 31
11. Jesus Walks on the Water—Mark 6:45-52 | 34
12. Jesus Teaches About True Purity—Mark 7:14-15 | 37
13. Jesus Rewards Improbable Faith—Mark 7:24-30 | 40
14. Jesus Warns Against Spiritual Arrogance—Mark 8:13-15 | 44
15. Jesus is the Messiah: Peter's Great Confession—Mark 8:27-30 | 48
16. Jesus Reveals His Glory—Mark 9:1-8 | 51

Contents

17 Jesus Helps Our Unbelief—Mark 9:23–24 | 55
18 Jesus Blesses Little Children—Mark 10:13–16 | 59
19 Jesus the "Good Teacher"—Mark 10:17–22 | 62
20 Jesus Enters the Temple—Mark 11:15–18 | 65
21 If You Do Not Forgive . . .—Mark 11:25–26 | 68
22 Render Unto Caesar—Mark 12:13–17 | 71
23 Jesus Teaches the Greatest Commandment—Mark 12:28–31 | 75
24 Jesus Will Return for His Elect—Mark 13:24–27 | 79
25 No One Knows the Hour—Mark 13:32–37 | 82
26 Calculation vs. Devotion—Mark 14:3–9 | 85
27 Jesus Institutes a New Covenant—Mark 14:22–25 | 88
28 Jesus, King of the Jews—Mark 15:1–5 | 91
29 Jesus Forsaken—Mark 15:33–34 | 94
30 And Peter—Mark 16:6–7 | 97
31 Jesus' Disciples Continue His Work—Mark 16:19–20 | 100

  Bibliography | 103

Introduction

THE GOSPEL OF MARK is a great introduction to the ministry and teachings of Jesus Christ. It was the first gospel written, and is compact and terse. Mark covers a lot of ground quickly, so we can get both the "big picture" about Jesus, and also some vivid details. Matthew and Luke both used Mark as a source document in writing their gospels, adding details and perspectives that Mark leaves out. Matthew is the reflection of an eyewitness. Luke is the *magnum opus* of a researcher. Mark is raw, primitive gospel. Eugene Peterson, translator of the Bible version *The Message*, said this about the Gospel of Mark in his inaugural address as professor of spiritual theology at Regent University:

> The Gospel of St. Mark is the basic text for Christian spirituality.... The entire canon of Scripture is our comprehensive text, the revelation that determines the reality that we deal with as human beings who are created, saved, and blessed by the God and Father of our Lord Jesus Christ through the Holy Spirit. But St. Mark as the first gospel holds a certain primacy.[1]

In this book, I've selected 31 passages from Mark's gospel. We will reflect on what Jesus preached about, who his friends and enemies were, how he related to God, to Jews, to gentiles, to women, to powerful authority figures, to the sick, the weak, and the poor. You'll hear Jesus' words from his own mouth. I'll fill in historical and theological details to give context to the readings.

1. Peterson, *Saint Mark*, 2.

INTRODUCTION

This is not simply a book of history or theology, though. My goal in these reflections is to invite you to consider Jesus and his teachings with fresh eyes. I'm not writing merely as a scholar, but as a pastor. My purpose is that this book gives you something to think about, to pray about, and to meditate on. I want you both to think and to believe as you read. As you reflect with me, I want you to have a greater understanding of the entire course of Jesus' life and ministry. I also want you to love him more.

S. H. Mathews

1

Jesus Calls Us to Follow Him
Mark 1:16–20

¹⁶ As Jesus walked beside the Sea of Galilee, he saw Simon and his brother Andrew casting a net into the lake, for they were fishermen. ¹⁷ "Come, follow me," Jesus said, "and I will send you out to fish for people." ¹⁸ At once they left their nets and followed him.
¹⁹ When he had gone a little farther, he saw James son of Zebedee and his brother John in a boat, preparing their nets. ²⁰ Without delay he called them, and they left their father Zebedee in the boat with the hired men and followed him.

THE FIRST PASSAGE WE will study together finds Jesus beginning his ministry in his home region of Galilee. Most of Jesus' ministry took place in the quiet setting of the villages and hills around the Sea of Galilee. As Jesus walked along the shore, he saw two sets of brothers, and called them to follow him. There is more meaning in this call than often meets the eye.

First, notice that Jesus found them fishing. They were busy at their family business. Simon and Andrew were fishing, while James and John were just about to start. Jesus didn't find idle men who followed him because they had nothing better to do. He called his early disciples away from an active, productive life of providing for themselves and their families. Discipleship carries a cost. Dietrich Bonhoeffer warned against "cheap grace" and urged us to count the cost of discipleship. We would do well to consider this. As the Gospel of Mark unfolds before us, we find that the call of Jesus is a call to full and total commitment.

Next, stop and think about what Jesus really meant when he said he would send them out to fish for people. These men were fishermen who ate and sold fish. What kind of fish? Dead ones, of course! Being caught in a fisherman's net was a death sentence for a fish. No catch-and-release fishing in Galilee! Even as Jesus called them to follow him, he indicated the nature of their ministry—they would call people to lay down their lives in the service of the Kingdom of God. When Jesus calls us to follow him, he does not call us simply to be religious do-gooders, but to give—and to call others to give—full commitment to Christ.

Take a look at whom Jesus calls here: two sets of brothers fishing on the Sea of Galilee. Two sets of rivals. Each day when they went out to fish, they competed for the catch. The rivalry between Peter and John is actually pretty well documented in the gospels. For example, in John 20:2-4, the two men were running to the empty tomb after hearing that Jesus had risen from the dead. John makes sure to tell his readers that he, not Peter, got to the tomb first! Peter and John had probably known each other from boyhood, and were (like most young Jewish men of their time), fiercely competitive. Yet Jesus called them both as equals. The call of Christ places us under subordination to him, and compels us to put aside human differences.

Finally, notice the emphasis Mark has placed on these men leaving their nets, families, and hired men. They are not taking a break from their work—they are quitting and walking away. Our own world is much more forgiving of this kind of behavior than first-century Galilee. In their world, everyone knew his or her place, and could measure how his or her status compared to someone else's. One's station in life was established by his or her birth, profession, tribe, gender, or some other factor over which each person had no control.

Jesus called these men to leave the familiar, the comfortable, and the acceptable to follow him. He called them to think of themselves differently than they ever had before, and to see themselves differently than others saw them. Jesus called them to take on a new identity.

There is much more to the call of Christ than meets the eye. Let's think about how the call to follow Jesus might apply to your life.

First, let's think of the cost of discipleship. Is there something that God is asking of you that you are holding back? Is there a price you don't want to pay? Are you trying to keep your day job of fishing while being a part time follower of Jesus Christ?

This leads us to a second question, about being caught like a fish. In Mark 8:34, Jesus said that if anyone wants to follow him, they must deny themselves, take up their cross, and come after him. The call of Jesus is a call to give ourselves up in radical obedience to God. Have you laid down your life, your desires at the feet of Christ? Are you willing to die to self and live for Christ?

Think about the rivalry between Peter and John. They competed with each other, and for all we know they may not have liked each other very much, but Jesus called them both to follow him. Is there someone with whom you can't get along? As a follower of Jesus, how can you work to put aside your own conflicts and follow Jesus together?

One more thing: think about the call of Jesus to these men to walk away from their roles in society, from the way they saw themselves. Jesus called them to think about themselves in a new way. Are you thinking of yourself in a way that hinders you from following Christ's call? Do you see yourself as too weak, too sinful, too shy, too uneducated, or too insignificant to pursue the call of Christ? Do your past actions, addictions, and relationships still define you? What about the way other people see you? Do you cling so tightly to the opinion of others about your place in the world that you can't just put down the nets and walk away? What will it take for you to change the way you see yourself and answer Christ's call?

As you read over this passage, pray for God to reveal his call to you. If you are already a follower of Jesus, then perhaps he is calling you to a specific ministry. Ask God to show you his call clearly, and to give you the strength to accept it. If you are not yet a follower of Jesus Christ, this call is for you. Acts 17:30 says that God is calling "all people everywhere to repent." That means that just as Jesus called these men by the Sea of Galilee to follow him, he is calling you to follow him as well. Our subsequent reflections on Mark's gospel will reveal much more about what it means to follow Jesus. Will you leave your nets behind and come after him?

2

Jesus Trades Places With Us
Mark 1:40–45

⁴⁰ A man with leprosy came to him and begged him on his knees, "If you are willing, you can make me clean."

⁴¹ Jesus was indignant. He reached out his hand and touched the man. "I am willing," he said. "Be clean!" ⁴² Immediately the leprosy left him and he was cleansed.

⁴³ Jesus sent him away at once with a strong warning: ⁴⁴ "See that you don't tell this to anyone. But go, show yourself to the priest and offer the sacrifices that Moses commanded for your cleansing, as a testimony to them." ⁴⁵ Instead he went out and began to talk freely, spreading the news. As a result, Jesus could no longer enter a town openly but stayed outside in lonely places. Yet the people still came to him from everywhere.

WORD HAD SPREAD ABOUT Jesus' ministry of healing and deliverance, so a leper came to him and asked for healing. He confessed faith in Jesus' ability to heal him, but he could never have expected Jesus to respond the way he did. Jesus loved him, touched him, then traded places with him! Let's take a closer look.

Come Follow Me

The man came to Jesus on his knees, believing that Jesus could heal him of his leprosy. Leprosy, known today as Hansen's Disease, was a particularly cruel affliction. It is a chronic bacterial infection which causes open sores on the skin, nerve damage, and muscle wasting. It is highly contagious. The Hebrew term for leprosy means "the scourge."[1] As the disease progressed, the victim would often lose fingers and teeth, along with large patches of skin. Leprosy could be a slow, painful death. Because it was so contagious, lepers were immediately quarantined outside of villages and cities, as Moses commanded in Leviticus 13:45–46. A diagnosis of leprosy was one of the most terrifying experiences of the ancient world. It often ruined entire families. If the husband and father contracted leprosy, he could not earn a living. It is no wonder that when word got out that Jesus was able heal diseases that this man came to seek his help. He did not simply want to be cured of a disease—he wanted his life back!

Notice Jesus' response—the New International Version of the Bible says he was indignant. Some other versions say "moved with compassion". Clearly, Jesus was upset, but why? Based on the way the leper approached him with humility and faith, Jesus was not indignant at the leper. In fact, he showed his compassion to the leper. So why was he indignant? I think Jesus was indignant at the sight of the man's suffering. This man was made in the image of God, loved by God, and was now suffering a terrible disease. Sin had so corrupted the universe that people suffered and died from cruel diseases. Though sometimes God feels far away, our suffering matters to Him.

The leper could never have guessed what would happen next. Jesus touched him! He touched a leper! How long had it been since this leper had felt the friendly touch of another person? He was unclean, and no one would touch him for fear of contracting his disease. But Jesus touched him. That's the deep love of Jesus. He did not simply heal this leper of his disease. He treated him like a person worthy of love and affection. To Jesus, no one is untouchable.

---

1. Davis, *Davis Dictionary of the Bible*, 470.

Jesus Trades Places With Us

We might puzzle over what Jesus did next, until we see it in light of his great love and compassion. He told the leper not to tell anyone what he had done, but to go and show himself to the priest. The Law of Moses commanded that a person healed from leprosy show himself to the priest for confirmation. When the priest confirmed the healing, he or she would offer a sacrifice of thanks to God. Jesus sent the man to the priest because in their society, only the priest could confirm his healing in a way that others would accept. The word of the priest was his ticket back to his life, his family, and his community. Jesus didn't simply heal this man's sickness; he set him on the path to wholeness. He gave this man his life back.

In a theme that will become common in Mark, the man did not go to the priest or keep Jesus' healing a secret, but told everyone what Jesus had done. He was exuberant with joy at the man who had loved him, touched him, and cleansed him. He could not help but speak! How can we keep it in if we have truly experienced the gracious love of God?

The former leper made such a commotion that Jesus could not enter any of the towns in the area without being mobbed, so he stayed out in the open. Look at what has happened here: before, the leper could not enter the town because of his sickness. He was excluded and shunned. Because Jesus healed him, he could reenter society, but then Jesus had to stay outside where the leper had been. Jesus has traded places with the leper. This is a foreshadowing of things to come—Jesus would take your place and mine on the cross, bearing the punishment for our sins. He came from heaven to earth so that we could be where he is. He came to trade places.

Think about your own life. Are you like the leper in this story? Do you feel cast out by those around you? Do you suffer with the pain of a physical illness? Do you long for love, affection, and friendship? If so, Jesus cares for you. He loves you, and reaches out to you. He wants you to know his grace and his love. He wants to trade places.

Maybe you can identify with Jesus in this story. Is there someone who needs to feel the love of God through your touch, to hear God's grace in your words? Can you reach out to them today?

3

Jesus Values the Soul Above the Body
Mark 2:1-12

A few days later, when Jesus again entered Capernaum, the people heard that he had come home. ² They gathered in such large numbers that there was no room left, not even outside the door, and he preached the word to them. ³ Some men came, bringing to him a paralyzed man, carried by four of them. ⁴ Since they could not get him to Jesus because of the crowd, they made an opening in the roof above Jesus by digging through it and then lowered the mat the man was lying on. ⁵ When Jesus saw their faith, he said to the paralyzed man, "Son, your sins are forgiven."

⁶ Now some teachers of the law were sitting there, thinking to themselves, ⁷ "Why does this fellow talk like that? He's blaspheming! Who can forgive sins but God alone?"

⁸ Immediately Jesus knew in his spirit that this was what they were thinking in their hearts, and he said to them, "Why are you thinking these things? ⁹ Which is easier: to say to this paralyzed man, 'Your sins are forgiven,' or to say, 'Get up, take your mat and walk'? ¹⁰ But I want you to know that the Son of Man has authority on earth to forgive sins." So he said to the man, ¹¹ "I tell you, get up, take your mat and go home." ¹² He got up, took his mat and walked out in full view

Jesus Values the Soul Above the Body

of them all. This amazed everyone and they praised God, saying, "We have never seen anything like this!"

MARK 1 ENDED WITH Jesus going on a preaching tour of the small towns around the Sea of Galilee. Here in Mark 2, Jesus has returned to Capernaum. Because of the miracles he did, both in Capernaum and all around the region, a great crowd gathered to see and hear him. Jesus' response was to preach the word to them. This "word" is the gospel—"The kingdom of God has come near. Repent, and believe the good news!" (Mark 1:15). This tells us something about Jesus' priorities right off the bat. The crowd may have gathered because of the miracles he performed, but Jesus kept his focus on the gospel.

The crowd was so large that the house was full, and people were pressed around the door and windows to hear Jesus teach. As he taught, four men began to dismantle the thatched roof above Jesus' head. Most houses in Galilee were made from clay, and would have a wood-framed roof with thatching. It could be removed and repaired with relative ease. The men lowered a mat, on which lay a man who could not walk. They passed him down to onlookers, who moved aside and laid him at the feet of Jesus.

Expectation was in the air! Some of these people had probably seen Jesus do miracles of healing. Certainly all had heard of the miracles described in Mark 1. They had been listening to the message of the gospel, but now the moment of truth had come. The paralyzed man was right before them, before Jesus, looking up, waiting. What would Jesus do? What could he do?

They certainly did not anticipate his response. Jesus looked the man in the eye and said "your sins are forgiven." This is problematic in several ways. First, Mark tells us that "when Jesus saw their faith", he forgave the sins of the paralyzed man. "Their faith" is the faith of the men who brought their friend to Jesus. In response to the faith they showed, Jesus imparted grace to the paralyzed man. Wait, though. We are forgiven for our own repentance—God responds to our own faith, not the faith of others. We must each come to God personally, right?

I believe that when Mark says that Jesus saw "their" faith, he is including the paralyzed man. He and his friends believed that Jesus could heal him, so they came. He was not brought against his will, purely on the basis of his friends' faith. He believed, and his friends believed, so together they came to Jesus for a miracle. But the miracle they got was not the miracle they expected!

The theologians in the audience—"teachers of the law"—immediately picked up on another problem. Only God can forgive sin. Sure, we can forgive each other for the wrongs we do to each other, but that does not really solve our sin problem. I can forgive you for lying to me, but you have still lied, and that violation of God's law stands. Only God can pronounce someone forgiven. For a man to say that he can forgive sin is blasphemy!

Notice that these teachers of the law are absolutely correct. No one—no parent, friend, or priest—can absolve people of their sins. That privilege is for God alone. Any man who claims to be able to forgive sins is a fraud.

Unless.

Unless, of course, that man is more than a man. If that man is God, then he has the power do what only God can do: to forgive sins. So now Jesus has put himself in quite a predicament. He has claimed for himself an authority that only God has, and all eyes are on him. Can he back up his claim? How can they trust that he has the power to forgive sin?

Jesus did not disappoint. He let his words sink in, then made his greater point: that his miracles and healings were performed to validate his message of the Kingdom. He said: "I want you to know that the Son of Man has authority on earth to forgive sins." He reached out to the man, took his hand, and stood him on his feet! The man who had never walked stood tall! The one who had spent his life lying on his back, looking up at everyone else could now look them in the eye. He was made whole again! He took his mat and walked out in amazement. Not only was he healed, he was forgiven!

Jesus Values the Soul Above the Body

One of the greatest morals of this story is that Jesus is more concerned about the soul than about the body. He raised this man to his feet, but one day, somehow, the man lay down and died. He caused blind eyes to see, but those eyes later closed in death. He healed lepers of their skin disease, but only for a season. Everyone Jesus healed still died. He fed the 5,000 and the 4,000, but they were hungry again later.

Jesus didn't come simply to heal people's bodies or to make them comfortable. He came to forgive people's sins—to put us in a right relationship with God. His miracles and healings were done to demonstrate his ability to perform his true mission—to heal the soul.

Think about your priorities. Do you demonstrate more concern for this world than for the next? Do you take better care of your body than of your soul? When these men brought their paralyzed friend to Jesus, the crowd saw the affliction of his body, but Jesus saw the great need of his soul for forgiveness. When you look at your life, do you focus on what is passing, or on what lasts forever?

4

Jesus Changes Everything
Mark 2:18–22

[18] Now John's disciples and the Pharisees were fasting. Some people came and asked Jesus, "How is it that John's disciples and the disciples of the Pharisees are fasting, but yours are not?"
[19] Jesus answered, "How can the guests of the bridegroom fast while he is with them? They cannot, so long as they have him with them. [20] But the time will come when the bridegroom will be taken from them, and on that day they will fast.
[21] "No one sews a patch of unshrunk cloth on an old garment. Otherwise, the new piece will pull away from the old, making the tear worse. [22] And no one pours new wine into old wineskins. Otherwise, the wine will burst the skins, and both the wine and the wineskins will be ruined. No, they pour new wine into new wineskins."

THIS TEXT FINDS JESUS and his disciples on a fasting day. There were several fasting days observed by some Jews in Jesus' day. The only day Jews were commanded to fast was on the Day of Atonement, but there were other fasts which were done in commemoration of significant events in the history of the Jewish people. It is not clear from the text which day this is, but it may have been the Day of

Atonement, because groups as diverse as the Pharisees and the followers of John the Baptist were fasting. Jesus and his disciples were not fasting, which caused some consternation among the people. They pointed out that other groups of Jews were fasting. Why not Jesus and his disciples?

Jesus responded to their question with three analogies: attending a wedding, patching a garment, and making wine. All three of his analogies make the same point: Jesus' arrival has changed everything. The world can never be the same again, because the Messiah has come. Life does not simply go on as before, because Jesus is Emmanuel, "God with us". If God is with us, then all of life is infused with divine meaning.

Jesus' first analogy is a wedding. Jewish weddings were extended times of feasting and celebrating with the bride, groom, and their families. It would be an insult to the host if one came to the wedding and did not eat. How much more of an insult if the groomsmen did not eat! Jesus told them that his followers were not fasting because they were the wedding party of the Messiah. Jesus' arrival was a time of celebration, not mourning. The time would come, however, when he would be absent, and then his friends would fast.

In his second analogy, Jesus described a common event in rural Galilee: patching a garment. We don't often think about fabric shrinking, because most of our clothing today is made industrially and is pre-shrunk. Fabric was handmade then, from the shearing of the sheep, to the spinning of the yarn on a drop spindle, to the weaving of the cloth which would be used for their simple clothing. A tunic was the result of hours of manual labor. Clothes were precious, and most people had only one, or perhaps two, sets of clothing. When a tear began, it must be patched quickly before the entire garment was ruined. A spare piece of cloth would be sewn over it. However, if the patch had not already been washed and shrunk, then when the tunic was washed, the patch would shrink and pull away. The problem would not be solved, but would be worse than before. It is interesting to notice that Jesus spoke to everyone here. Making clothing was women's work in the highly stratified society of first-century Galilee. Many rabbis refused to teach women, but Jesus used analogies that everyone could understand. He wanted his entire audience—men and women, rich and poor, young and old—to hear and understand his message!

The third analogy related to making wine. Wine is fermented grape juice, of course. The Jews would store grape juice in bags made from the stomachs or skins of sheep. It sounds strange to us, but nothing went to waste! During the fermentation process, the juice would give off gasses that would cause the skin to expand, and every so often, the wine-maker would release these gasses. New wineskins were elastic enough to expand and contract, but older, brittle skins would burst. Jesus' analogy about putting new wine—wine that is still fermenting—into old skins would make perfect sense to his audience.

What is the point of these analogies? What was Jesus trying to say? Remember, the people asked why he and his disciples were not observing a particular religious ritual—fasting. These analogies make the point that Jesus came to turn the world on its head. The Jewish rituals of old were performed to prepare people for the arrival of their Messiah. Now that the Messiah had come, the meaning of these rituals did not fit God's activities. Because the Messiah was standing right in front of them, there was no use in performing rituals that were intended to anticipate his arrival!

Long ago, the astronomer Ptolemy taught that the earth was the center of the universe. Everyone believed him, and this was the foundational assumption of astronomy. However, as astronomers tracked the movement of planets, they realized that something was not quite right. In order to maintain the idea that the earth was the center of the universe, they had to devise strange theories about the movement of planets. Then Copernicus realized that the sun, not the earth, was the center of our universe. The change in perspective was tremendous! Suddenly, astronomy made sense! Likewise, since the Messiah has come, the meaning behind things like fasting, prayer, and worship becomes clear.

Jesus did not do away with religious observances like fasting. He had fasted (Matthew 4:1–11), and his followers fasted (Acts 13:2).

They met daily in the temple to pray (Acts 3:1). Jesus' first disciples continued to live as Jews, but these actions took on new meaning because Jesus had fulfilled them. In short, Jesus changes everything.

What has Jesus changed in your life? How do you see the world differently because of Jesus Christ? Does your religious life consist of empty rituals that have lost their meaning? Worse, are you the center of your own universe, instead of Jesus Christ? Jesus changes everything. What has he changed for you?

5

Why was Jesus Angry?
Mark 3:1-6

Another time Jesus went into the synagogue, and a man with a shriveled hand was there. ² Some of them were looking for a reason to accuse Jesus, so they watched him closely to see if he would heal him on the Sabbath. ³ Jesus said to the man with the shriveled hand, "Stand up in front of everyone."

⁴ Then Jesus asked them, "Which is lawful on the Sabbath: to do good or to do evil, to save life or to kill?" But they remained silent.

⁵ He looked around at them in anger and, deeply distressed at their stubborn hearts, said to the man, "Stretch out your hand." He stretched it out, and his hand was completely restored. ⁶ Then the Pharisees went out and began to plot with the Herodians how they might kill Jesus.

As Mark's account of Jesus' life and ministry proceeds, Jesus' revolutionary ministry and teaching bring him into conflict with the religious establishment. This conflict will continue to escalate throughout Jesus' ministry. In the end, the jealousy of certain Jewish religious leaders from the sects of the scribes, Pharisees, and Sadducees will lead to Jesus' death. In this passage, the conflict is just beginning to take shape. Jesus has gone into a local synagogue on the Sabbath. A man with a birth defect—a shriveled hand—was present. Some people who were jealous of the attention Jesus was getting from the people were also there, watching to see if there was an opportunity to trip him up.

Jesus saw the trap they had laid for him, so he took the initiative. He called the man with the withered hand to the center of the room. All eyes were on Jesus and on this poor crippled man. Jesus asked his opponents a simple question: is it lawful to do good on the Sabbath? Of course it is, but they had no answer for Jesus. Their hearts were too hard to admit that Jesus was right.

At this point, Jesus showed an emotion that Mark has not yet depicted: he became angry. Why was Jesus—the incarnation of the God of love—so angry? Mark tells us: he was "deeply distressed at their stubborn hearts." Put yourself in the scene for a moment. Imagine you are the man with the shriveled hand. This is not simply an inconvenient or embarrassing physical flaw. This is a life-altering disability that has had a profoundly negative impact on your life, your family, and your sense of identity.

With a withered hand, a man can't work like other men. He has to do with one hand what other men do with two. Who would hire a one-handed man to do labor for the same wage as a strong, healthy man? This disability had certainly hurt him financially, and it probably hurt him in other ways, as well. Think about this: who would marry a man who can't do a full days' work for a full days' pay? In a society in which men are honored for their accomplishments, who would respect a man who can't do what other men can do? The suffering caused by his withered hand went much deeper than the physical level. This man was hurting deeply because of the suffering brought on by living in a fallen world.

What made Jesus so angry? The people looking to trap him were the religious leaders, the Pharisees. They were the people who were supposed to tell others about God's love. They were supposed to show that God cares for the poor, the outcast, and the brokenhearted. But they did not care about this man at all. His suffering did not move them. To them, he was simply a pawn in their attempt to hold on to their positions of religious leadership. That's what made Jesus angry.

Jesus healed the man, not to prove anything to the Pharisees, but because he loved this man. He saw his suffering, and he took it from him. He made him a whole man—a man who could stand tall in his society and earn a living wage. Jesus demonstrated the love of God for a person who was hurting, and he was angry at those who did not.

Let's think about our lives. We are surrounded by hurting people, struggling with physical, emotional, mental, and spiritual needs. We may not have the power to speak a word and take these troubles from them, but we have the power to show the love of God, even in their suffering. Who do you know who is hurting? Do you care—really care—about their pain? What will you do to ease their heartache and show them that God loves them and has not forgotten them?

6

Jesus Can Pardon all Sins but One
Mark 3:28–30

> [28] Truly I tell you, people can be forgiven all their sins and every slander they utter, [29] but whoever blasphemes against the Holy Spirit will never be forgiven; they are guilty of an eternal sin."
>
> [30] He said this because they were saying, "He has an impure spirit."

JESUS' GREAT MESSAGE OF the Kingdom is that God forgives sin. God has sent His Son, Emmanuel—God with us—to heal the schism between God and humanity. Up to now in Mark's gospel, Jesus has been healing all kinds of diseases and forgiving all kinds of sins, so we are surprised to come upon an exception to the universal scope of the forgiveness offered by God in Christ.

Notice that Jesus starts with a focus on God's grace: "people can be forgiven all their sins and every slander . . ." God's focus is on forgiveness, not on condemnation. The list of sins God can forgive is infinite; the list of sins He cannot forgive has only one entry on it: blasphemy against the Holy Spirit.

Sometimes people wonder if they have committed the unpardonable sin. They wonder, "Am I out of reach of God's grace?

Have I done something God cannot forgive?" What does it mean to blaspheme the Holy Spirit? How can one know if one has committed this "eternal sin"?

Let's take a look at what the Holy Spirit does, so we can figure out what it means to blaspheme God's Spirit. Here are a few examples of the work of the Holy Spirit: In Mark's gospel, the Holy Spirit descended on Jesus at his baptism (1:10), and drove Jesus into the wilderness to be tempted (1:12). Luke tells us that the Spirit anointed Jesus to preach the gospel to the poor (4:18), and that Holy Spirit is a gift from the Father (11:13). John's gospel says that the Spirit gives life (6:63) and that the Holy Spirit will guide Jesus' followers into all truth (16:13). The Holy Spirit convicts the world of sin, righteousness, and judgment (John 16:7-11). No one can come to the Jesus unless the Father, through the Holy Spirit who gives life, draws him or her (John 6:63-65). The Holy Spirit gives Jesus' disciples power for witness (Acts 1:8).

There are other examples, but these are enough to give us an idea of what the Holy Spirit is up to. The Holy Spirit magnifies Jesus Christ, and convicts people of their need for Jesus. The Holy Spirit brings people to Jesus for forgiveness of their sins, and empowers them for witness and ministry.

If this is true, then what does it mean to blaspheme the Holy Spirit, and why is this sin unpardonable? To blaspheme the Holy Spirit is to reject the drawing of the Holy Spirit to Jesus Christ. When the Holy Spirit draws, calls, and convicts a person, and that person finally and utterly rejects God's grace, this is the blasphemy of the Holy Spirit. Why is this sin unpardonable? It is unpardonable because in rejecting the Holy Spirit, one rejects the only means of forgiveness of sins—God's grace. The person who rejects the witness of the Holy Spirit to Jesus Christ has cut himself or herself off from the forgiveness that God offers in Jesus Christ.

How can a person know if he or she has blasphemed the Holy Spirit? Paul said that when people are confirmed in their sins, God turns them over to a reprobate mind (Romans 1:28). He also describes people whose consciences are seared as with a hot iron (I Timothy 4:2). When the Spirit stops drawing a person, this person may have utterly rejected the Spirit's witness to Christ. As long as the conscience testifies to a person's need for grace, the Spirit is at work in his or her life. Whatever sins someone may have committed, as long as the Holy Spirit continues to draw him or her to Christ, there is forgiveness available.

Someone once said that the role of the Holy Spirit is to comfort the afflicted and to afflict the comfortable. That is, the Spirit brings peace to those who are suffering, but agitates those who are comfortable with themselves to greater depths of obedience. Can you see the comforting and convicting work of the Holy Spirit in someone's life? How can you be used by God to help them respond to the Spirit's drawing?

7

Cultivation of the Heart

Mark 4:13–20

[13] Then Jesus said to them, "Don't you understand this parable? How then will you understand any parable? [14] The farmer sows the word. [15] Some people are like seed along the path, where the word is sown. As soon as they hear it, Satan comes and takes away the word that was sown in them. [16] Others, like seed sown on rocky places, hear the word and at once receive it with joy. [17] But since they have no root, they last only a short time. When trouble or persecution comes because of the word, they quickly fall away. [18] Still others, like seed sown among thorns, hear the word; [19] but the worries of this life, the deceitfulness of wealth and the desires for other things come in and choke the word, making it unfruitful. [20] Others, like seed sown on good soil, hear the word, accept it, and produce a crop—some thirty, some sixty, some a hundred times what was sown."

JESUS TAUGHT IN PARABLES very often. A parable is a way of telling a particular truth using simile—"the Kingdom of Heaven is like . . .". Most parables in the gospels are not interpreted for us by Jesus or by the gospel author. It is left to the reader to interpret them, and it is assumed that the reader can do so. Indeed, most of Jesus' parables are not very difficult to interpret. Mark presents us with a parable, however, that requires some explanation.

The parable was straightforward: a man went forth to sow seeds. He used the broadcast spreading method, in which handfuls of seed are thrown all around. Seed fell everywhere. Some seed fell on the footpath, and birds came and ate it. Some seed fell on rocky ground. It sprang up, but because the soil was so rocky, there was no room for a strong root system, so they died. Some seeds fell in thorny places, and after they germinated, the weeds and thorns choked them out. Finally, some seed landed in the field which the farmer had prepared for it. It took root, grew, and bore fruit.

Jesus' disciples asked him to explain the parable of the soils, so he set out a pattern of interpretation. This parable is an allegory: the seed is the Word of God, cast out to the whole world. Sometimes the Word falls in barren, beaten-down paths. Satan comes and takes the Word away. These are people who are so blinded by sin that the Word of God finds no place in their lives. They reject God's message immediately.

Other people receive the Word, but only superficially. They are the rocky soil. When the Word enters their ears, they rejoice in what they are hearing. However, it never really enters their hearts and takes root. As soon as obeying the Word becomes difficult, they fall away, moving on to the next interesting thing they hear.

The next group of people is interesting to Jesus. He gives more explanation to this group than to the first two. This is the thorny soil—a heart in which the Word of God has to compete for space with the weeds of anxiety, greed, and double-mindedness— "the worries of this life, the deceitfulness of wealth and the desires for other things". This person hears the gospel, but never allows God's message of grace to transform his or her heart. He hears the gospel, but he still wants other things. She hears the gospel, but she still worries about life. He cannot fully accept the gospel of a poor, wandering rabbi because he is deceived by wealth. Soon enough, the gospel is choked out.

Finally, there is the seed that fell into the field. The field represents people who hear the Gospel, receive it, and allow it to take root in their lives. The result is that they bear fruit. Jesus used specific figures—thirty, sixty, and one hundred times—to make a point, not to offer a calculation. Some Christians bear more fruit than others, but all true Christians should bear fruit.

What is the difference in the soils? Why was the soil in the field so fruitful? The farmer had prepared it. The soil was tilled, rocks and thorns were removed. Weeds were pulled. Before sowing the seed, the farmer would spend days or weeks removing obstacles, so the seed could grow. If you and I want the Word of God to take root in our hearts, we will have to remove the rocks and weeds. Several are mentioned in this parable, such as anxiety, greed, and double-mindedness. There are others: anger, lust, and a variety of attitudes and behaviors that choke out the seed of the Gospel in our lives.

Understand, cultivating your heart is not about becoming good enough before you come to Christ, or about doing enough good works to become holy by your own effort. Instead, it is about cooperating with God to root out elements from your life that get in the way of the gospel's life-transforming message. It means rejecting moral filth, forgiving those who hurt you, honoring God with your time, money, and possessions. David said it like this: "Who may ascend to the hill of the LORD? Who may stand in his holy place? He who has clean hands and a pure heart, who does not lift up his soul to an idol or swear by what is false" (Psalm 24:3–4). This is a picture of a cultivated heart which has room for the seed of the Word to grow.

What rocks and thorns are choking out the seed of the Word in your life? What habits draw you away from obedience to Christ? What thorns compete with God for your love? What anxieties prevent you from trusting God? What possessions own you? If you want to bear fruit, you must cultivate your heart. How can you start today?

8

Jesus Calms the Sea
Mark 4:35–41

³⁵ That day when evening came, he said to his disciples, "Let us go over to the other side." ³⁶ Leaving the crowd behind, they took him along, just as he was, in the boat. There were also other boats with him. ³⁷ A furious squall came up, and the waves broke over the boat, so that it was nearly swamped. ³⁸ Jesus was in the stern, sleeping on a cushion. The disciples woke him and said to him, "Teacher, don't you care if we drown?"

³⁹ He got up, rebuked the wind and said to the waves, "Quiet! Be still!" Then the wind died down and it was completely calm.

⁴⁰ He said to his disciples, "Why are you so afraid? Do you still have no faith?"

⁴¹ They were terrified and asked each other, "Who is this? Even the wind and the waves obey him!"

AFTER TEACHING EXTENSIVELY THROUGH parables, Jesus invited his disciples to get into the boat and go "to the other side". No specific destination is named; they are simply going to "the other side". In fact, where they are going is not immediately important for the lesson Jesus wants to teach them. Rather, the significance of the journey is the experience they will have along the way.

Mark usually keeps the action moving, and writes only the basic aspects of an event. In this passage, however, Mark provides some important details that give us clues to what Jesus is doing with his disciples.

First, they got into the boat with Jesus and left the crowd behind. A journey to the other side with Jesus is not a mass event. It is not for anonymous groupies, but for Jesus' intimate followers. Where Jesus wants to take them, he must take them individually. They would each experience the coming storm in a very personal way.

Second, they took Jesus in the boat "just as he was". Jesus had been preaching for most of the day, and simply stepped into the boat to cross over. He had nothing to bring, no bag to pack, to plans to set in order. Jesus, as he was, was enough.

Third, there were other boats with them. Who were in these other boats? Mark does not say, so we are left to speculate that these boats were populated by those who followed Jesus at a distance. They enjoyed the sermons and the miracles, but they were not intimate followers of Jesus. The seed had landed in their lives (to borrow from Jesus' earlier parables), but had not taken deep root.

When the journey across the Sea of Galilee was underway, a "furious squall" arose—a terrible storm common on the Sea of Galilee as the wind rushed down the mountains to the water. I'm speculating here, but I imagine that this storm drove away the other boats, so only Jesus and his disciples were left on the sea.

As the disciples struggled at the oars, Jesus slept on a pillow. What a contrast! Twelve men fighting for their lives, while one man sleeps peacefully. Jesus had taught all day, and was now tired. Finally, fearing death, they awoke Jesus with a question: "don't you care if we drown"?

Looking back on this story, we have the omniscient perspective of a narrator. We know what Jesus is going to do, because the story is familiar to us. However, in the moment of the storm, surrounded by danger and filled with terror, the disciples asked the logical question of God: "don't you care"? Two thousand years have passed, and we, Jesus' disciples, still ask the same question. When our boat is rocking and nearly swamped, doesn't God care? Does he care if we have cancer? Does he care that I lost my job? That my marriage is on the rocks? That I've been used and rejected? That the growing ache in my heart for real companionship and affection is tearing me apart?

So they woke Jesus up. Jesus did not rebuke them for interrupting his slumber. Instead, he rebuked the wind and the waves, and the sea became calm. In our times of doubt and fear, Jesus is not angry with us. It is no sin to be afraid in a sinking boat in a stormy sea. Nevertheless, Jesus then turned to his bewildered disciples and asked two simple questions: "why are you so afraid?" and "do you have no faith?" I don't think Jesus spoke these words harshly. There was no anger in his voice. Mark saves the word "rebuke" for Jesus' words to the sea, not to his friends. These are simple questions, asked in the ultimate teachable moment. Jesus asked his friends to trust him.

What emotion did this elicit in these men? We are surprised to read it: terror. They were afraid of the wind and the waves, but they were terrified when they got a real glimpse of Jesus' power. Who is this man, that even the wind and waves obey him? This is no wandering do-gooder rabbi, no simple moral teacher. They loved Jesus, and had committed to follow him, but they were just beginning to realize that he was much more than they ever imagined. Jesus had to bring them out to the sea, to the storm, to the very edge of death itself, to get them to see him for who he truly was. He had to bring them to the other side.

What about you? Has God invited you to some "other side" experience? Have you been in the sinking boat in the stormy sea, asking God: "don't you care?". Perhaps your storm is an invitation to take a closer look at Jesus Christ. Perhaps it's not enough to hear his teachings. Perhaps he is bringing you to the point where you need him desperately.

9

Jesus Sends His First Missionary
Mark 5:18–20

[18] As Jesus was getting into the boat, the man who had been demon-possessed begged to go with him. [19] Jesus did not let him, but said, "Go home to your own people and tell them how much the Lord has done for you, and how he has had mercy on you." [20] So the man went away and began to tell in the Decapolis how much Jesus had done for him. And all the people were amazed.

AFTER JESUS CROSSED TO the other side of the Sea of Galilee with his disciples, he cast a legion of demons out of a man who lived in a cemetery by the seashore. People from nearby villages were amazed to see the man sitting, dressed, and in his right mind. They feared the power that Jesus demonstrated, and begged him to leave.

As he got into the boat to leave, the former demoniac "begged to go with him". He had been delivered from mental, emotional, and spiritual torment, and wanted nothing more than to become a disciple of Jesus. Notice the contrast between this man and Jesus' disciples. They were Jews, he was a gentile. They were mostly respectable Galilean tradesmen and fisherman, he was a social outcast. Jesus called them to follow him, but this man asked to follow Jesus.

We might expect that Jesus would accept this man as a disciple. He would be a great witness to Jesus' power and mercy. Indeed, this was exactly the plan Jesus had for this man, but not as one of his immediate disciples. Jesus sent him to his own people—to those in the ten gentile villages known as Decapolis who had known of his fearsome reputation in the cemetery.

Though his exposure to Jesus was brief, this man had everything he needed to serve as Jesus' missionary to the gentiles. His message was his own witness: "how much the Lord has done for you, and how he has had mercy on you." He needed no further instruction or education. His own life story was his gospel to the gentile nations. A Jewish rabbi named Jesus had cast many demons out of him and had delivered him from bondage.

This message was enough. As he went through Decapolis proclaiming his deliverance, the people were amazed. They had seen and heard of this man as a wild demon-possessed lunatic. Word had spread not to pass through the cemetery for fear of the violent man who lived among the tombs. His body still bore the scars of the shackles and chains that could not hold him, as well as the wounds he had inflicted on himself. Now he stood before them, sane and giving a clear and verifiable witness of God's great work in his life. While Jesus was preaching the gospel of the Kingdom of God in Galilee, this man was proclaiming God's grace in the gentile region on the other side of the lake.

His witness was not wasted. In Mark 7:31, Jesus returned to the region of Decapolis. This time, however, the people did not beg him to leave. Instead, they brought him a man who was deaf and mute, and Jesus healed him. As a result of Jesus' ministry in the area, the people were "overwhelmed with amazement", and exclaimed that Jesus "has done everything well" (Mark 7:37).

What was the difference between Jesus' two visits to Decapolis? The first time, he did a great work, but the people begged him to leave. The second time, when word spread of his arrival, people came to hear him teach, and they brought him someone to heal.

The difference was the witness of the missionary Jesus had sent! Just as John the Baptist prepared the way for Jesus' ministry to the Jews, this unnamed missionary prepared the gentiles of his region to receive Jesus' ministry.

Remember Jesus' parable of the soils in Mark 4:13–20? The farmer cast the seed everywhere, but some soil had been cultivated to receive it, so it took root and bore fruit. That's what this missionary did for the people of his region. His testimony of God's goodness and power prepared their hearts to receive Jesus' ministry. The first time they met Jesus, their hearts were rocky and weedy, and there was no room for him. The second time, after seeing and hearing of his grace in the life of this missionary, they rushed to meet him, hear him, and see his power firsthand. That's the difference a cultivated heart makes.

What is your mission field? What work of grace has God done in your life that you can show to those around you? How can you help to prepare people to hear and receive God's grace? Just as Jesus sent this man to his own people with a powerful message of God's love, he also sends us to testify of his goodness. Will you go?

10

Jesus Sends Out the Twelve
Mark 6:7–13

⁷ Calling the Twelve to him, he began to send them out two by two and gave them authority over impure spirits.

⁸ These were his instructions: "Take nothing for the journey except a staff—no bread, no bag, no money in your belts. ⁹ Wear sandals but not an extra shirt. ¹⁰ Whenever you enter a house, stay there until you leave that town. ¹¹ And if any place will not welcome you or listen to you, leave that place and shake the dust off your feet as a testimony against them."

¹² They went out and preached that people should repent. ¹³ They drove out many demons and anointed many sick people with oil and healed them.

AT THE BEGINNING OF his ministry, Jesus called his twelve disciples to follow him. He found them absorbed in the ordinary business of life—fishing, working in a tax booth, sitting under a tree. He interrupted their lives with his authoritative presence, and as they left their business to follow him, they increasingly saw the power of God in him. Now he gave them his power and sent them out to the world.

Notice several aspects of what Jesus did. First, he sent them out in pairs—"two by two". No disciple went out alone. Each man had a brother, a friend, a helper. Their ministry was not a solo endeavor; rather, they ministered in the name of Jesus just as they followed him—as a family.

Notice also that Jesus gave them authority over impure spirits. In Mark 1, Jesus amazed the crowd at the synagogue at Capernaum by demonstrating his authority over evil spirits. Now he has given this same authority to his disciples. Their ministry was to look like his ministry.

He instructed them in the overall pattern of their ministry: they were not to bring any money or food or spare clothing. They could bring only what they were wearing, their shoes, and a walking stick. In short, Jesus sent them out to serve, and asked them to trust him. They could not bring bread to eat, or money to buy food. They had to trust that God would provide their meals. Nights in the desert are cold, so travelers would often bring an extra tunic if they were not sure of a room for the night. The disciples would have to forgo this, trusting that God would house them.

Because they would have to trust God to provide for them through other people, Jesus also laid out some ground rules for accepting hospitality. When they arrived at a house and were welcomed, they were to stay in that house until they left town. If they were offered better accommodations in a wealthier house, it would be offensive to leave their poorer host. They were to trust God to provide, then accept what he provided with gratitude.

What if someone rejected their message? Jesus had that one covered, too. He told them to walk away. "Shake the dust off your feet as a testimony against them." There were plenty of people ready to hear God's good news, so when Jesus' disciples came upon people who did not want to believe, they should just keep moving.

With these instructions, the disciples set out in pairs. Wherever they went, they imitated what they had seen Jesus do: they preached that people should repent, because the kingdom of God was at hand. They cast out demons and healed the sick with the authority Jesus had given them. Two by two, Jesus' disciples multiplied his ministry throughout Galilee.

There are several lessons to learn as we follow Jesus today. The first is that we don't follow him alone. The American idea of radical individualism is foreign to the gospel. In life, and in ministry, God's plan always involves the companionship and fellowship of other disciples.

Notice also that Jesus gave them his authority. They did not use their own wisdom or charisma or knowledge, but the authority of God. Their ministry was authoritative because they knew Jesus. In Acts 4, Peter and John were arrested and brought before the council of Jewish elders. They were uneducated fishermen, but they spoke with power and authority. The Jewish elders said that "they had been with Jesus." What a compliment—to look and sound like Jesus!

Third, look at the trust involved in ministry. When we follow Jesus and reach out to others to encourage them to follow Jesus also, we trust that God will provide for our needs and for the results of our ministry. If people welcome us and the gospel, we share it—no matter who they are. If they reject the gospel, we can move on in ministry to other receptive people.

Finally, look at the results of their ministry. They preached, cast out impure spirits, and healed the sick. Our ministry today may look different than this in form, but not in substance. Jesus calls his followers to work together in ministries that magnify his gospel.

If you are a follower of Jesus, put yourself in the disciples' sandals for a moment. Are you going out in Jesus' authority to do his work, or just following him? After the disciples followed for a while, Jesus put them to work. He gave them everything they needed, and sent them out. It's the same with you and me. Jesus does not call us simply to passively follow him, but to actively take the gospel to those around us, showing his love in our actions and our words. Will you trust God enough to go, and not just to follow?

11

Jesus Walks on the Water
Mark 6:45-52

⁴⁵ Immediately Jesus made his disciples get into the boat and go on ahead of him to Bethsaida, while he dismissed the crowd. ⁴⁶ After leaving them, he went up on a mountainside to pray.
⁴⁷ Later that night, the boat was in the middle of the lake, and he was alone on land. ⁴⁸ He saw the disciples straining at the oars, because the wind was against them. Shortly before dawn he went out to them, walking on the lake. He was about to pass by them, ⁴⁹ but when they saw him walking on the lake, they thought he was a ghost. They cried out, ⁵⁰ because they all saw him and were terrified.
Immediately he spoke to them and said, "Take courage! It is I. Don't be afraid." ⁵¹ Then he climbed into the boat with them, and the wind died down. They were completely amazed, ⁵² for they had not understood about the loaves; their hearts were hardened.

MARK 6 HAS A theme of seeing, but not believing. The people in the synagogue at Nazareth saw Jesus and heard about his miracles, but did not believe in him because he was too familiar to them. They knew him, and they knew his mother, so he could not be the Messiah. Herod saw and heard the message of John the Baptist, but did not believe because he preferred to live in sin with his brother's wife. The disciples had seen Jesus' previous miracles, but did not believe he could feed the crowd of 5,000 men, plus women and children. And now, in this text, the disciples see Jesus walking on the water, but do not believe because they are superstitious and terrified.

In this text, Jesus has just fed the 5,000, and sent his disciples away in a boat so that he could dismiss the crowd and go pray alone. This had been his original purpose in going to the wilderness—to pray after hearing of the death of John the Baptist, his cousin and friend. Late at night, after he finished praying, Jesus was alone on the land, while his disciples struggled at the oars of their boat. The wind was against them.

The Sea of Galilee is actually a large lake surrounded by high hills. From the "mountainside" where Jesus prayed, he "saw the disciples straining at the oars." Look at the contrast here. On the one hand, we see the disciples crowded into a boat—straining, sweating, pulling with all their might to get to the place where Jesus had sent them. On the other hand, we see Jesus kneeling peacefully on the mountainside, watching their efforts and praying to the Father. Keep this contrast in mind as you read the rest of the passage.

Shortly before dawn—the disciples had been rowing all night—Jesus came out to them, walking on the lake. He acted as if he would simply walk by them, and made sure they saw him. And see him they did! They cried out in terror, believing that a ghost or spirit was visiting them. Sailors have always been a superstitious lot, and apparently, fishermen on the Sea of Galilee were no different.

But these men should have been different. They had been given the authority of Jesus, and had cast out demons, two-by-two. If they had seen firsthand their authority over evil spirits in pairs, why should twelve of them together be so terrified? They had just seen Jesus multiply five pieces of bread and two fish to feed thousands of people. Why should their minds immediately revert to fear? Before these men met Jesus, we have to assume that their lives were very ordinary—fishing, working, collecting taxes. But since they became followers of Jesus, they had seen God's supernatural power at work all around them. Now, tired and tested, when they saw something they did not understand, their first assumption was that it was a malevolent spirit.

Sometimes we do this, but in a different way. As we evaluate the circumstances of our lives, we see ourselves in the boat, straining at the oars. We are tired, and feel like we are getting nowhere—like life is an endless cycle of working, eating, and sleeping. The people around us seem to be trapped in the same struggle, like the disciples in the boat. We forget that God is at peace above us, watching.

Then something happens. Some change comes into our lives: the loss of a job, a change in our patterns of life, or an issue with our family's health. How often do we immediately assume that it is something negative? I've seen many followers of Jesus (and of course I've done it myself!) cry out in terror at what turned out to be God at work in their lives. Why do we so often immediately think the worst, even when we know that God is at work?

How can you look at changes and challenges as opportunities for God to show His power, rather than as situations that show the loss of God's power?

12

Jesus Teaches about True Purity
Mark 7:14–15

¹⁴ Again Jesus called the crowd to him and said, "Listen to me, everyone, and understand this. ¹⁵ Nothing outside a person can defile them by going into them. Rather, it is what comes out of a person that defiles them."

THE JEWISH RELIGION IN the time of Jesus had developed a very detailed code of ritual purity. They believed that what a person touched had a profound impact on that person's standing with God. Touching sinners, dead animals, or dead people would make a Jew "unclean", and he or she would lose standing with God until he or she were ritually pure again. The same applied to eating. If a person ate a food which was considered unclean, then they could not think of themselves as being right with God.

It was inevitable that every Jew, even the most conscientious, would touch unclean people and things from time to time, so intricate purity rituals were established to wash away the effects of "uncleanness." In Mark 7:1–4, Mark tells us that the Pharisees and scribes had come to Jesus from Jerusalem and were appalled to find Jesus' disciples eating without first undergoing the prescribed purity rituals. Mark describes in detail how the "Pharisees and all the Jews" practiced the washing not only of their hands, but of other things which may be made unclean, such as cups, pitchers, and even furniture.

The Pharisees confronted Jesus in Mark 7:5, and asked him why his disciples ate with unwashed hands. The issue is not really about clean hands. There is a deeper question implied here. Jesus was becoming a well-known rabbi, travelling throughout Galilee and into Judea, gathering large crowds. He had begun to wield significant influence. Didn't he care about purity? Didn't he teach his followers to be clean and pure before God?

That's the real issue here. The Pharisees were obsessed with keeping their right standing before God by staying ritually pure. We often criticize the Pharisees today, and indeed, we have good reason, based on their behavior in the gospels. Jesus himself criticized them frequently (for example, in his response to their question, he calls them hypocrites). However we may fault their behavior, their underlying motivation was a good one—to be right with God. Their mistake was trying to be right with God through their own external works, rather than through the inward change that true faith brings. Still, we can't fault them for wanting to be pure in the eyes of God.

After Jesus rebuked the Pharisees in verses 6–13, he spoke the words under consideration. He underscores the importance of this teaching with his opening words: *"Listen to me, everyone, and understand this."* Jesus called his audience to attention before he taught—he wanted to be sure they understood what he was going to say about purity. The Pharisees' real question had been "don't you care about purity? Don't you teach your followers to be pure?" The answer is a resounding "yes!", but Jesus did not teach his followers that they could be made pure by washing their hands, or by not eating the wrong things. In Jesus' mind, this is not purity at all. True purity is something else entirely.

Jesus said *"Nothing outside a person can defile them by going into them."*. In the Genesis account of creation, God created everything, and stopped frequently to remark that what He had created was good. Everything God made, in and of itself, is good. There is nothing we can eat, no germ we can get on us, that alienates us from God. Purity is not biological, it is spiritual. Our standing with God is not based on the contents of our stomach, but on, to borrow a phrase from Martin Luther King, Jr., "the content of our character".

Jesus told his audience: *"Rather, it is what comes out of a person that defiles them."* We are defiled by our actions and by our words. The motivations of our hearts are revealed in our actions (vs. 21–23), and these actions declare whether we are pure or defiled. A defiled heart leads to words and actions of sin. Jesus lists several of these in verses 21 and 22. A pure heart reveals itself in actions and words of grace.

This is a really liberating truth. The Pharisees were bound to a tradition of ritual purity. Purity could be lost at any time, and regained only by performing the right ceremonies. What does this say about their view of God? It says that God is only pleased with a person if they happen to have conducted the right ritual at the right time. What kind of God is this? This is not the God Jesus describes throughout the gospels.

The God Jesus describes as his Father looks at the heart of every man and woman. He judges people by their actions—the fruit of their hearts' desires. Jesus indeed wanted his followers to be pure, but not by washing their hands. He wanted his followers to have pure hearts. Pure hearts would show in holy living.

What about you? What kind of heart do your words and actions reveal? Do they show a heart that has been changed by God's grace and love? Throughout the gospels, Jesus calls people to repent—to change their hearts—because God's kingdom is at hand. Does your heart show evidence of repentance?

13

Jesus Rewards Improbable Faith
Mark 7:24–30

²⁴ Jesus left that place and went to the vicinity of Tyre. He entered a house and did not want anyone to know it; yet he could not keep his presence secret. ²⁵ In fact, as soon as she heard about him, a woman whose little daughter was possessed by an impure spirit came and fell at his feet. ²⁶ The woman was a Greek, born in Syrian Phoenicia. She begged Jesus to drive the demon out of her daughter.

²⁷ "First let the children eat all they want," he told her, "for it is not right to take the children's bread and toss it to the dogs."

²⁸ "Lord," she replied, "even the dogs under the table eat the children's crumbs."

²⁹ Then he told her, "For such a reply, you may go; the demon has left your daughter."

³⁰ She went home and found her child lying on the bed, and the demon gone.

IN THIS STORY, JESUS has left Galilee and traveled to the region of Tyre, to the northeast. Tyre was a gentile city on the coast of the Mediterranean Sea. Jesus accepted the hospitality of some host there—he entered a house, and wanted to enjoy a quiet visit.

However, his fame had gone before him even to Tyre, and his presence could not be kept secret for long.

A woman came to Jesus with a request, and a most puzzling conversation followed. As soon as she heard he was in Tyre, the mother of a little girl with an impure spirit came to Jesus. We call her the Syro-Phoenician woman, for the place of her birth. She came and fell at Jesus' feet—a sign of her sincere and humble request. Her desire was straightforward: she wanted Jesus to "drive the demon out of her daughter".

This is nothing new to Jesus. We have seen him cast out demons before—as many as several thousand at one time. Usually, when people came and fell at Jesus' feet, he accommodated their requests. Remember Jairus in Mark 5:22? Think of the contrasts between Jairus and this Syro-Phoenician woman: Jairus was a Jew; she was a gentile. Jairus was a man; she was a woman. Jairus was a leader in the synagogue—a respectable leader of the Jews; she was a foreigner. Yet they both came to Jesus and fell at his feet to beg him to help their daughters. When Jairus asked for Jesus' help, Jesus immediately began to follow him to his house. But this time, it's different.

Jesus' response to the Syro-Phoenician woman looks insulting at first. He told her that it is not fitting to take food from the children (the Jews) and give it to the dogs (the gentiles). In fact, "gentile dog" was a common insult in Jesus' day. Did Jesus really return this woman's trust and humility with an insult? Did she ask him to help her daughter, only to have a common insult thrown at her? I don't think so, and I'll tell you why.

The woman's response does not indicate that she felt insulted, so there must be more going on here than the written word can convey. I think perhaps Jesus said this with a smile and a wink. Both he and she knew the common conflicts between Jews and gentiles—perhaps he is gently teasing her, breaking the tension of the moment. She did not react if he had rebuked her harshly, so we should understand Jesus' words in terms of his mission.

She came right back at Jesus—"yes, but even the dogs get crumbs from the table." She understood that God is the God of all people, not only the Jews. She may be a gentile, but she is a child of God, and had as much right to ask for help as any Jew.

Jesus was delighted with her answer! Whatever he was trying to convey in his jest earlier, she "got it". He told her that because of her answer, she could go home to her daughter. Her request had been granted. Indeed, she went home to find her daughter resting safely, the unclean spirit having left her.

Let's discuss this story. Just before he came to Tyre, Jesus had a heated conflict with the scribes and Pharisees in Galilee. After healing this woman's daughter, he would bypass the region of Galilee and travel to Decapolis, a region consisting of ten gentile cities. There, he will heal a deaf-mute, and the gentiles there will exclaim "He has done all things well!" (Mark 7:37).

Jesus is expanding his mission to the gentiles in this section of Mark. Where the Jews were becoming hard-hearted, the gentiles were open to his work. The scribes and Pharisees wanted to argue, but the gentiles wanted God's grace. Jesus was the Savior not only of the Jews, but of the world, and his mission to the gentiles demonstrates God's love for all people.

What can we learn from this story? Two lessons come to mind. The first is the expanding scope of Jesus' ministry. Jesus was a Jew, the Jewish Messiah. He came to the Jews in fulfillment of prophecy to save God's people from their sins. But he was not the Savior only of the Jews, but of the world. He came to be the Savior of Tyre and Decapolis as well as Galilee and Judea. Gentiles are not an afterthought in the mind of God. We have always been part of God's plan of salvation.

The second lesson that presents itself here relates to the puzzling nature of Jesus' words to the woman. I've seen many interpretations of this passage that take offense at Jesus' words. They see Jesus alternatively as a male chauvinist pig insulting a woman, or as a provincial Jew expressing disdain for gentiles. Of course, neither interpretation is true. What should we do when we come upon a difficult text in the Bible? How should we receive words we don't understand? I think we should always read Jesus' words in light of his mission. Everything Jesus said is a function of who he is, and his mission. If I don't understand what he said, I should consider these words in light of what Jesus is all about—bringing people to God.

We do not always understand everything we read in the Bible. Even after years of academic study, scholars puzzle over the meaning of texts. This is fine. We are not required to have God figured out, but simply to live in faithful obedience.

What about you? Do you have a sense of God's universal mission? Do you show God's love to "outsiders"? Do you "receive with meekness the implanted Word" (James 1:21), trusting in God's grace and love even when you do not understand everything you read? When we can trust God's heart and show His love to those who are different than us, we are closer to the Kingdom than ever.

14

Jesus Warns Against Spiritual Arrogance

Mark 8:13–15

[13] Then he left them, got back into the boat and crossed to the other side. [14] The disciples had forgotten to bring bread, except for one loaf they had with them in the boat. [15] "Be careful," Jesus warned them. "Watch out for the yeast of the Pharisees and that of Herod."

THIS PASSAGE FINDS JESUS and his disciples in a boat, crossing the Sea of Galilee. Two significant events have just occurred that led to Jesus' cryptic warning about the "yeast of the Pharisees and that of Herod".

In Mark 8:1–10, Jesus performed a feeding miracle. Previously, he had fed over 5,000 Jews in Galilee. Here, he fed 4,000 gentiles in the region of Decapolis. After each of these feeding miracles, the disciples had gathered baskets full of leftover food. Jesus had not only provided sustenance; he had provided abundance. After this second feeding miracle, Jesus got into a boat and crossed the Sea of Galilee to the town of Dalmanutha[1].

1. For many years, biblical scholars questioned the existence of the village

Jesus Warns Against Spiritual Arrogance

In Mark 8:11–12, Jesus arrived at Dalmanutha, and was immediately accosted by a group of Pharisees. They "came out and began to argue with Him, seeking from Him a sign from Heaven, to test Him." The Pharisees probably had not heard of the feeding miracle which had just occurred, but knew of Jesus' reputation as a teacher and of his previous conflicts with the Pharisees. They thought of him as a troublesome traveling teacher who should be opposed. When they heard that he had landed on their shore, they came out to challenge him.

The irony here is clear: the Pharisees demanded a miracle from a man who had just demonstrated his divine power a few hours earlier by miraculously feeding 4,000 people!

Jesus was grieved in his spirit. He did not argue, and he certainly did not give them a sign. Instead, he got into the boat and left. I can imagine the Pharisees congratulating themselves: they had run off the troublesome Jesus!

This brings us to Jesus' statement in the boat: "beware of the yeast of the Pharisees and that of Herod." What is the "yeast" of which Jesus speaks? He is using this symbolic language because he had just created bread for the multitudes. I believe that this "yeast" is spiritual arrogance. Let's explore this concept a moment.

The crowds Jesus fed had gathered not to challenge him, but to listen to him. They stayed out in the open places for days at a time to listen to Jesus talk about the Kingdom of God. These people—the ones with open minds and hearts—saw and received the benefit of Jesus' miraculous power. The Pharisees stormed up to Jesus and demanded a sign from heaven. In their pride, they demanded what Jesus had so often freely given to those who simply believed.

King Herod was in the same boat. In Mark 6, he had a birthday party for himself. He invited all the most important people in his region. There was wine and food, and entertainment. Salome, the daughter of Herodias, Herod's new wife, danced an erotic

---

of Dalmanutha, since the exact location had never been discovered. In 2013 an archeologist documented the discovery of a village he believes to be Dalmanutha. See Dark, *Archaeological evidence for a previously unrecognised Roman town near the Sea of Galilee*.

dance. In the presence of his guests, Herod offered her any lavish gift she should ask. Guided by her mother, she asked for the head of John the Baptist on a platter. John was in Herod's prison, but Herod did not want to kill him. Mark 6:26 tells of Herod's regret: "And although the king was very sorry, yet because of his oaths and because of his dinner guests, he was unwilling to refuse her." He sent the executioner to John's cell immediately.

In both cases, the "yeast" is arrogance. In their arrogance, the Pharisees have challenged Jesus repeatedly. Herod's pride caused him to boastfully offer any gift the girl could want, and then his pride would not allow him to refuse her request.

Jesus' symbolic use of the word "yeast" is significant. Yeast is a living culture added to dough to make bread rise. Yeast is alive; a tablespoon of yeast contains millions of live bacteria. Likewise, arrogance takes on a life of its own. Pride is an animating force in the human heart. This is why John wrote in 1 John 2:16 that there are three things that are in the world that lead us to sin: the lust of the flesh, the lust of the eyes, and the pride of life.

Yeast also permeates the dough. Bakers do not use a lot of yeast. A pinch is enough for a loaf of bread. The live yeast bacteria feed on the dough, growing and multiplying. Likewise, a little arrogance permeates our lives, feeding off every imagined slight and offense. No wonder Jesus told his followers to "beware"—a little arrogance can grow quickly!

Yeast also changes the bread. The only difference between a thick, chewy pizza crust and a fluffy loaf of bread is a little yeast. Yeast makes the dough rise. In the same way, arrogance changes us. When we give in to arrogance, we are the Pharisees, challenging God and demanding things from Him (much like the health-and-wealth prosperity gospel in our day). Without this arrogance, we are the people gathered to listen to Jesus, and to receive his grace and feeding.

What about you? Is the "yeast of the Pharisees and of Herod" working its way into your life? Are there areas in your life in which you make demands of God, rather than trusting Him? Is your speech boastful, instead of humble? Do you see Jesus as a challenge, rather than as a friend? Be careful to root arrogance out of your life as soon as you find it. Like yeast, a little arrogance will permeate your life, and it will change you.

15

Jesus is the Messiah: Peter's Great Confession

Mark 8:27-30

²⁷ Jesus and his disciples went on to the villages around Caesarea Philippi. On the way he asked them, "Who do people say I am?"
²⁸ They replied, "Some say John the Baptist; others say Elijah; and still others, one of the prophets."
²⁹ "But what about you?" he asked. "Who do you say I am?"
Peter answered, "You are the Messiah."
³⁰ Jesus warned them not to tell anyone about him.

THE JESUS WE HAVE met so far in Mark's gospel is outward-focused. He is on a mission, preaching, teaching, and healing. In his conflicts with the scribes, Pharisees, and Sadducees, he is confident, assertive, and strong. He seems to care little what others think of him, and has certainly made no attempt to cater his ministry to the wishes of his admirers or his enemies. He has walked away from adoring crowds, and stood firm in the face of opposition. The Jesus of Mark's gospel is not broody or introspective. Until now.

Now, on the road to Caesarea Philippi, Jesus stops his disciples and asks two questions. It is not insignificant that Jesus asks these questions about halfway through Mark's gospel. Jesus gave his disciples time to watch and listen, to see his miracles and hear his teachings, before asking for a verdict. But he did, indeed, ask for a verdict. Halfway through his ministry, it is time to evaluate: did people see God in Jesus?

Jesus starts with a public relations question: "Who do people say I am?" As the disciples mixed and mingled with the public apart from Jesus, they had heard the gossip about him. Some said that he was John the Baptist, raised to life again, after Herod had executed him. This is not surprising. Their ministries were similar in style and focus. They were cousins, in fact. Others associated Jesus with the great prophetic tradition of Israel—perhaps he was even Elijah! In 2 Kings 2:11, Elijah was taken to heaven alive in a chariot of fire. Because he never died, many Jews believed that Elijah would come back to earth one day. Could Jesus be Elijah, sent down from heaven to deliver Israel from Roman oppression?

Having heard the popular theories, Jesus asked a more personal, pressing question: "who do you say that I am?" Here and now, on the side of the road, face to face, Jesus asked his disciples to render a verdict. They had seen and heard his ministry and lifestyle for a couple of years now. It was time to make up their minds.

Peter spoke up on behalf of the group: "You are the Christ". Matthew's gospel adds "the Son of the Living God." This is a bold, clear statement of Jesus' messianic identity. It is the first clear, unequivocal confession of faith in Jesus as Messiah in Mark's gospel. Jesus' response to this confession is surprising at first. He warned them not to tell anyone about him. Now that they clearly understood that he was the Messiah, they must allow him to reveal himself on his terms and in his time.

I spoke to a man the other day who said that Jesus was a great moral teacher, in a class with the Buddha, Mohammed, and Lao Tzu, the founder of Taoism. There have been many great moral teachers, including in our lifetimes: Ghandi, Martin Luther King,

Jr, and the Dali Lama. Jesus came, according to my friend, to teach moral lessons.

What do you think? Was Jesus simply a great teacher like many others? Jesus certainly did not think so. He stated repeatedly, boldly, and clearly, that he was the Son of God. He called on people to trust him to save their souls. He said that those who had seen him had seen the Father. He told people that he was going ahead of them to heaven to prepare a place, and that he would return to take his people home one day. With these and many other statements, Jesus made the bold, clear claim that he was God. And he asked for a verdict.

We cannot simply accept the moral teachings of Jesus—forgive your enemies, help your neighbor, give to the poor—and overlook his insistence on his own divinity. Jesus claimed to be God, so what do we do with that?

C.S. Lewis wrestled with this question. He came up with three plausible answers[1].

The first option is that Jesus claimed to be God, but knew he was not. Jesus was just a man like any other, but with a special gift of charisma to gather followers and make speeches. He claimed to be the Son of God for the sake of theatre, prestige, or power. Jesus is a liar.

The second option is that Jesus was not the Son of God, but he really thought that he was. He was, again, a man like any other, but he truly believed that he was God's Son. We have mental hospitals for people like this. This represents a detachment from reality that is staggering. Jesus is a lunatic.

The third option is that Jesus claimed to be the Son of God because he was the Son of God. His claim to divinity was backed up by the power and authority of his teachings, by the miracles he performed, and ultimately by his resurrection from the dead. Jesus is Lord.

As you study the life of Jesus through this book and others, you will have to come to terms with who he is. Is he a liar, a lunatic, or the Lord? Who do you say that he is?

1. Lewis, *Mere Christianity*, 56.

16

Jesus Reveals His Glory
Mark 9:1–8

And he said to them, "Truly I tell you, some who are standing here will not taste death before they see that the kingdom of God has come with power."

² After six days Jesus took Peter, James and John with him and led them up a high mountain, where they were all alone. There he was transfigured before them. ³ His clothes became dazzling white, whiter than anyone in the world could bleach them. ⁴ And there appeared before them Elijah and Moses, who were talking with Jesus.

⁵ Peter said to Jesus, "Rabbi, it is good for us to be here. Let us put up three shelters—one for you, one for Moses and one for Elijah." ⁶ (He did not know what to say, they were so frightened.)

⁷ Then a cloud appeared and covered them, and a voice came from the cloud: "This is my Son, whom I love. Listen to him!"

⁸ Suddenly, when they looked around, they no longer saw anyone with them except Jesus.

AFTER JESUS' QUESTION AND Peter's confession, Jesus made a prediction: some of the men standing before him would not die before they saw the kingdom come with power. In Jesus' world, this was a loaded statement. There were many conceptions floating around of what the Kingdom of God would look like. The most common was an expectation that the Jews would break the shackles of Roman bondage and establish a kingdom with their own king. The line of David would once again rule Israel from David's holy city, Jerusalem. There were groups of Jews like the Zealots who actively engaged in guerilla warfare against Rome, and while most Jews bore Roman occupation patiently, they longed for the restoration of the kingdom. Jesus even had a Zealot for a disciple, named Simon.

The Messiah they awaited for such an earthly kingdom was necessarily a political and military leader. Every so often a "Messiah" would arise—Judas Maccabeas, Bar Kochba, and others—who would lead the Jews to varying degrees of military victory over Roman might in this or that province. Then these messiahs would die and time would march on. The Kingdom had not come.

So when Jesus said that some of these men would live to see the Kingdom of God coming with power, we can imagine what may have been in their minds.

Mark does not give us long to wait before he records what Jesus intended. Just six days later, Jesus took Peter, James, and John up onto a mountain. These men were Jesus' "inner circle", and were frequently alone with Jesus when he performed miracles or explained parables. On the mountain, Jesus was "transfigured". That is, his figure was transformed. Mark describes him: a radiant glow shone forth from Jesus, making his clothes "dazzling white". Moses and Elijah stood on the mountain, talking with Jesus.

Why Moses and Elijah? These men—Jesus, Moses, and Elijah—represent the fulfillment of God's redemptive purpose for humanity. Moses was the lawgiver. God gave the law, with all its ordinances and regulations, to set an impossibly high standard for humanity. To be righteous, one would have to obey the law in every detail. Because they could not keep the law perfectly, the Jews had to bring animal sacrifices to atone for their sins. They brought special offerings for special sins as needed, and every year, on the Day of Atonement, they would fast and bring animal sacrifices to

God to atone for their sins. These offerings were repeated annually because they were imperfect and incomplete. There was never perfect, final forgiveness. Just more offerings next year. On the mountain, Moses represents the law.

Elijah was one of the greatest of the prophets. On this mountain with Jesus, he represents the prophetic tradition of Israel. The prophets spoke about many things, but the most important was the Messiah. The prophets spoke to a people bound to the law and its sacrifices and told them that one day, God would send the Messiah to release them from these obligations. The Messiah would save them.

On the mountain, Moses represents God's giving of the law to show people the impossibility of being righteous through their own efforts. Elijah represents the hope that God would save His people; that He would make them righteous. What does Jesus represent? Jesus is the fulfillment of the law and the prophets. Jesus is the Messiah the prophets foretold, who would release the Jews from bondage to the law by forgiving them for their sins and making them righteous.

Taking in this scene, it would be easy to forget Peter, James, and John. Peter finally spoke up, as he usually did. He offered his analysis of the situation (it is good to be here), and his proposal for future (he could build tents for Jesus, Moses, and Elijah). In the grandeur of this moment, Peter has nothing better to offer than his approval and some light construction work! This is a perfect example of the futility of human efforts at righteousness!

There has been another Presence, invisible on the mountaintop. Now God the Father speaks in response to Peter's pronouncement: "This is my Son, whom I love. Listen to Him!" The voice of God from heaven removes all doubt about Jesus' identity as the Messiah. Peter has confessed Jesus as the Messiah, Moses and Elijah have appeared with Jesus on the mountain, and now the voice of God Himself has declared: Jesus is the Son of God.

The Kingdom of God was not what they expected at all. The Kingdom of God is not an earthly kingdom with laws, an army, and a palace. Jesus Christ is the Kingdom of God. When he preached "the Kingdom of God is at hand", he was talking about himself. The King from the line of David had returned indeed! The king is the Kingdom!

This is a turning point in Mark's gospel. The first half of Mark introduces us to Jesus—his teaching and preaching, his miracles, his arguments. Now we are forced into a crisis of identity: who is Jesus really? The second half of Mark takes on a faster tempo, a darker tone. His identity revealed, Jesus begins his march toward the cross.

Jesus is the fulfillment of all of God's purposes for saving us. Has he fulfilled these purposes in your life? Can you say with Peter that Jesus is your Messiah?

17

Jesus Helps Our Unbelief
Mark 9:23–24

²³ "'If you can'?" said Jesus. "Everything is possible for one who believes."
²⁴ Immediately the boy's father exclaimed, "I do believe; help me overcome my unbelief!"

WE JUST SAW JESUS transfigured on the mountaintop. We saw him standing with Moses and Elijah. We heard the voice of God declare that Jesus is His beloved Son. It was a glorious, radiant moment of God's revelation. Now, that moment has passed as quickly as it came, and we are back in the real world. As Jesus walked down the mountain with Peter, James, and John, they talked about the Messiah's role in the Kingdom of God. Jesus revealed things to them that they had never heard.

Then they came back to the road where the other disciples were waiting. There was a crowd—a mob, really. Angry words were shouted back and forth. The scene was getting ugly. Something was happening, and the disciples were right in the middle of it. While Jesus and a few chosen disciples were on the mountain with Moses, Elijah, and God the Father, the rest of the disciples were on the road with an angry mob! What happened?

A father had brought his young son to Jesus' disciples to have a demon cast out of him. The disciples tried, but could not do it. The boy was brought to Jesus, and the demon convulsed and threw him to the ground. The father explained to Jesus that the boy had suffered from birth. "If you can do anything" he said, "take pity on us and help us."

Jesus told the father that all things are possible for one who believes. With faith, nothing is impossible. The boy's father immediately exclaimed that he did believe, then added the marvelous words "help me overcome my unbelief."

Help me overcome my unbelief. Can you see the power in this simple request? This is the cry of a heart that believes, but struggles with doubt. This is a faith that trusts, but wavers in dark moments. Yet even in the midst of doubt and wavering, this is a faith that trusts Jesus to fill in the lack, to make the faith strong enough to see God through to His answer.

All too often, we see faith as an all-or-nothing proposition. We read the Bible's injunctions to believe without doubting, as we find in James 1, and we see no room in faith for doubt, for questions, for hesitation. We even have a name for those who doubt: "Doubting Thomas". Yet, beneath it all, every one of us struggles with faith. Not one of us always believes God fully for everything we need, without a hint of doubt. We all have unanswered questions.

This father is an honest man, and his cry expresses my situation, and perhaps yours. "I believe, but I need to believe more. I trust God, but I struggle with doubt. Help me overcome my unbelief!"

Think about the great men and women of the Bible who are known for their faith. Moses led the people out of Egypt, through the Red Sea, and through their wilderness wanderings. He gave them the law, and is a great hero of the Jews. Yet he often doubted and cried out to God that something was not right—that his plight was not fair. When God appeared to him in a burning bush to send him back to Egypt, he doubted and did not want to go. He led the Israelites to the border of the Promised Land, but he was not permitted to enter it because of his rash anger in a time of crisis.

Elijah was a great prophet. He stood up to 450 prophets of Baal on Mount Carmel, called down fire from heaven, slaughtered the prophets of Baal, then outran the king's horses for miles and miles. After that he went alone into the wilderness and prayed that God would kill him because he felt all alone.

These are great men—the men who stood with Jesus on the mountain of his transfiguration—and they doubted. We honor them for their faith, and rightly so, but their faith was not without struggle. In their darkest moments, exhausted and alone with their thoughts, they questioned the God who had called them. Was His purpose worth their suffering? Would He really deliver them? Were they on the right track? Had God forgotten them?

If God can use and honor people like Moses and Elijah (not to mention Abraham, Peter, Hannah, Samuel, David, and many others whose faith in God was a struggle), then He can use you, even with your imperfect faith. On the road, the father asked Jesus to help his unbelief. In response, Jesus cast the demon out of his son. Remember Doubting Thomas? The other disciples had seen Jesus resurrected, and told Thomas about it. He said that he would believe when he could see what they had seen. A week later, Jesus appeared to them all in an upper room. Jesus walked straight over to Thomas. Instead of a rebuke, he offered Thomas his hand. "Look at my hands. Look at my side. Touch me and see me."

Jesus was not angry with this father for his doubt, nor with Thomas. Nor with you. This father asked for help to overcome his unbelief, and Jesus healed his son. Thomas wanted proof, and Jesus showed him the fresh wounds from his crucifixion. If you struggle with doubt, Jesus makes the same offer: "I'll help your unbelief. Watch me."

In a previous reflection, we saw that Jesus himself is the coming of the Kingdom of God with power. In this passage, he is the solution to questions and doubts. He did not come to find those with perfect faith; he came to help us who struggle with unbelief.

In what areas are you struggling with your faith? Do you feel guilty because you have honest questions and doubts? Don't give in to guilt over this. Call on Jesus to help you overcome your doubts. He does not condemn you.

18

Jesus Blesses Little Children
Mark 10:13-16

¹³ People were bringing little children to Jesus for him to place his hands on them, but the disciples rebuked them. ¹⁴ When Jesus saw this, he was indignant. He said to them, "Let the little children come to me, and do not hinder them, for the kingdom of God belongs to such as these. ¹⁵ Truly I tell you, anyone who will not receive the kingdom of God like a little child will never enter it." ¹⁶ And he took the children in his arms, placed his hands on them and blessed them.

MARK 10 STARTS WITH Jesus engaged in a weighty theological dispute with the Pharisees. The topic was as difficult then as now: divorce. In an extended passage, Jesus responds to the Pharisees' questions, interprets the Law on the issue, then follows up with his disciples. We see Jesus the theologian discussing an important issue with important religious leaders. We could hang a sign over the whole scene: "do not disturb".

But they were disturbed. They were interrupted by parents bringing little children to Jesus so he could bless them. The disciples recognized the significance of the discussion that was going on, and began to shoo the children away. When Jesus saw this, "he was indignant." Jesus rebuked his disciples, explained a theological principle of the kingdom of God, and then welcomed the children to himself and blessed them.

What principle of the kingdom of God did Jesus teach his disciples? The kingdom of God belongs to those who receive it as a little child. This was a more revolutionary principle than we can imagine! Place yourself into the shoes of the Pharisees with whom Jesus had been disputing. They had studied the Law from childhood, with the goal of gaining a mature understanding of God. Likewise, Jesus' disciples had been following Jesus for quite some time, listening to his teaching and watching the miracles he performed. They had given up their lives to follow Jesus, and now they heard him say that access to the Kingdom of God is based on child-like faith?

Let's observe something important Jesus said here. He was talking about receiving the Kingdom of God. Receiving the kingdom is entering it. He was talking about the faith to become a Christ-follower, to enter the kingdom. Without simple trust in Jesus, no one can enter his kingdom. The kingdom belongs to those who receive it like children receive gifts from their parents—with simple trust.

Receiving, or entering, the kingdom is not the same as living in it. In theological terms, we make a distinction between the doctrine of justification, which is how we enter the kingdom of God through repentance and faith in Jesus, and the doctrine of sanctification, which discusses how we live in the Kingdom of God and become more like Jesus Christ. Jesus was calling for simple, child-like faith to enter the kingdom, but he also calls men and women to follow him through a life of obedience, reflection, and devotion. We may enter the kingdom as little children, but we should also grow up in it, as mature adults.

After saying this, Jesus blessed the children. He held them in his arms, laid his hands on them, and pronounced blessings over them. One of my most prized rewards of ministry is a Thanksgiving card I received from a little girl just shy of her fourth birthday. She had become attached to me, and would always come and speak to me at church. She would hug me and sit on my lap, telling me about whatever was important to her. I invited her family to my farm so she could play with my baby goats. Her mother was helping her write Thanksgiving cards. Her card to me said simply: "I am thankful for you because you are kind, you hug me, and you are letting me see your goats." This is more important than any theological debate I could engage in.

This passage says so much about following Jesus, both through Jesus' words and through his example. Following Jesus is a matter of receiving his kingdom through childlike faith, then living in increasing faith, obedience, and maturity. But the most important things in the kingdom are not doctrines, weighty theological questions, or jockeying for positions of prominence. The most important things are grace, love, and blessing those around us. I think this is what Jesus meant when he said that the most important commandments are to love God and to love others. If we can get these things right, the rest will fall into line.

19

Jesus the "Good Teacher"
Mark 10:17-22

[17] As Jesus started on his way, a man ran up to him and fell on his knees before him. "Good teacher," he asked, "what must I do to inherit eternal life?"

[18] "Why do you call me good?" Jesus answered. "No one is good—except God alone. [19] You know the commandments: 'You shall not murder, you shall not commit adultery, you shall not steal, you shall not give false testimony, you shall not defraud, honor your father and mother.'"

[20] "Teacher," he declared, "all these I have kept since I was a boy."

[21] Jesus looked at him and loved him. "One thing you lack," he said. "Go, sell everything you have and give to the poor, and you will have treasure in heaven. Then come, follow me."

[22] At this the man's face fell. He went away sad, because he had great wealth.

AFTER JESUS' THEOLOGICAL DISCUSSION with the Pharisees and his blessing of the children, Mark brings the discussion back to the kingdom of God in a powerful way. As Jesus was traveling, a man ran up and asked him a question. Previously, the Pharisees had come and asked a question, which constituted a challenge to Jesus' authority. This question is different: "what must I do to inherit eternal life?" In asking his question, the man calls Jesus an honorific title: "good teacher". The man is not challenging Jesus, but asking a sincere question. This is not the context for a debate, but for a meaningful conversation about the kingdom of God.

Jesus' response to the young man's question has puzzled commentators throughout the years—"why do you call Me good? No one is good except God alone." Perhaps it is best to interpret Jesus' words here in the same manner as his response to the Syro-Phoenecian woman in Mark 7:27, in which he appears to call her a "gentile dog." Jesus' response there was probably tongue-in-cheek, and likewise here, he was not denying his deity, but pointing out the implications of the man's own words. He called Jesus good, but was he prepared to call him God?

Jesus' next words are quite interesting. He cited for the man six of the Ten Commandments, but substituted "do not defraud" for the tenth commandment: "do not covet". Two things are of note here. First, Jesus only cited the commandments that deal with the way people relate to each other. The first four commandments address the relationship of people to God, and Jesus does not include these. Second, he substituted the commandment against coveting other peoples' possessions with a simple prohibition against defrauding others. The reason for this substitution will become clear in verse 22—the man had many possessions, and wanted to keep them. Jesus' listing of these particular commandments sets the man up to respond as he does—that he has kept these specific commands from his birth. That is, outwardly, with the exception of covetousness, he has obeyed all the "big" rules. He has not stolen, or murdered, or committed perjury. He has honored his parents. He did not seem to catch the missing reference to coveting what other people have. Perhaps he was relieved that Jesus skipped that one!

Jesus looked on this man with love. It is important to remember when reading the words of Jesus, that he is the love of God, sent to humanity. He is God with us, sent to redeem, and not to condemn. Just as he loved the little children, so he also loved this young man. Mark has repeatedly pointed us to the compassion Jesus felt for the hungry crowds, for the sick, and for the demon-possessed. In love, Jesus called this man to follow him. His injunction was simple: let go of all that you possess, and follow me. The reward would be "treasures in heaven". Notice that Jesus' words here are addressed to one specific man. He does not call everyone to sell everything we have and give the money to the poor. The question, however, is what we would do if he did ask this of us. Would you relinquish your earthly possessions in obedience to God, or would you go away grieving, unwilling to let go of the things you have acquired?

The man had asked the question, but was not prepared for the answer. In fact, he probably expected Jesus to tell him that on the basis of all the rules he had kept from his youth, he was already in the Kingdom of God. What Jesus asked was too high a price to bear. He went away grieving, weighted down by his desire for the things of the world. Here is a question for you: do you own your things, or do your things own you? There is a simple test: if you can't let something go, it owns you.

20

Jesus Enters the Temple
Mark 11:15–18

¹⁵ On reaching Jerusalem, Jesus entered the temple courts and began driving out those who were buying and selling there. He overturned the tables of the money changers and the benches of those selling doves, ¹⁶ and would not allow anyone to carry merchandise through the temple courts. ¹⁷ And as he taught them, he said, "Is it not written: 'My house will be called a house of prayer for all nations'? But you have made it 'a den of robbers.'" ¹⁸ And the scribes and chief priests heard it and sought how they might destroy Him; for they feared Him, because all the people were astonished at His teaching.

Mark 11 depicts Jesus' "triumphal entry" into Jerusalem. Jesus arrived in Jerusalem to shouts of "Hosanna in the highest!", and songs of worship. Pilgrims placed their cloaks, as well as palm branches, on the road before him. For one brief moment, it seemed that Jesus would be honored as the Son of God. In an anticlimactic scene, Jesus went to the temple and looked around a moment, then left because it was already evening (Mark 11:11). The scene is also ominous: Jesus would be back. He came for a purpose, and it would be completed.

The next day, Jesus entered the Temple and went on a rampage. He pushed over the tables of the money changers, scattering and mixing their coins. He chased away those who were buying and selling offerings. Why? The law required that an offering be *brought* to the Lord, but bringing an animal on a journey to Jerusalem was inconvenient. It was much easier to simply buy one upon arrival. So the court of the Temple had become a bazaar, where one could buy doves, sheep, and other offerings. People from different regions came, and money changers converted currency (at a price, of course) to the correct coins for the temple offering. Religion became convenient and commercialized—not unlike our own day. The spirit of the sacrifice was lost.

This is why Jesus acted so uncharacteristically violent in this scene. How else could he get his point across?

Mark tells us that people were carrying merchandise through the temple. Instead of a holy place of worship, it was a convenient thoroughfare to carry goods to market. The temple had no more significance for many people than any other public space where goods were hawked. Rather than walk around the Temple, they just went straight through. Jesus also ran these people off.

Of course, these events did not go un-noticed! When Jesus had caused enough of a scene to generate a crowd, he started to teach: the house of God is a house of prayer for all the nations. It represents the presence of God among His people. But these people had turned the temple and its sacrifices into a way to profit off of each other's easy-believism. They robbed God and robbed each other. Their religion did not honor God, and it did not edify people. This is what happens when religion comes to be oriented around the desires of people, rather than God. Religion becomes easy, because the focus is placed on the things that are already important to us. We may maintain the outer appearance of sacrifice to God, but in reality, we serve only ourselves. When this happens, we see other people, and even God Himself, as a means to whatever end we are seeking. In our own day, the prosperity gospel—the idea that God's greatest desire is to give people health and wealth—is an example of this kind of thinking. Another example is self-righteous legalism, in which people try to justify themselves through their own actions, rather than relying the grace of God.

Who was responsible for maintaining the order and decorum of the temple? Whose job was it to keep the focus on God? Who had let the Temple become a common marketplace? The chief priests and scribes were entrusted with this duty, and on their watch, the Temple had lost its meaning as the sanctuary of God. They feared Jesus all the more because the multitudes were "astonished" at his teaching. When Jesus spoke to the crowds, they heard the wisdom of God. His words rang with the very resonance of heaven. Their own words fell like lead, empty and devoid of the power of God.

The contrast between Jesus and the religious establishment was so great that they began to look for ways to destroy him. The Pharisees and Herodians (religious and political groups, respectively) had already been looking for ways to destroy him, so the "perfect storm" was brewing. Jesus' ministry caused the necessary conflict to lead him to the cross, so that God's ultimate purpose would be fulfilled for the redemption of humanity.

There is always a temptation to make faith in God easy, cheap, and convenient. Are there areas in your life in which you are taking spiritual shortcuts? Is the temple of your heart bustling with activity but devoid of the presence of God? What do you need to do to clear it out? What tables in your own life need to be kicked over?

21

If you do not forgive . . .
Mark 11:25-26

²⁵ And when you stand praying, if you hold anything against anyone, forgive them, so that your Father in heaven may forgive you your sins.

THINK FOR A MOMENT—WHAT is the greatest force in the universe? What force has more power than any other? It's not a nuclear reactor or a hydrogen bomb. It's not wind, solar, or petroleum energy. It's grace.

Grace? Powerful? We don't think of grace as powerful, we think of it as, well, graceful. We think of grace as quiet, still, whispered in hushed tones. We don't think of power. But consider this question: what is the greatest need in the universe? We constantly hear politicians, philosophers, economists and others talking about what we need to make life better. What do we really need to solve the greatest problem of the human condition?

The greatest problem of the human condition is sin, and the only solution to that problem is grace. Therefore, grace is the most powerful force in the universe! We could solve every human problem known to man—poverty, violence, racism, war, hunger—and still be left with the greatest human problem—sin. Our greatest need is to be forgiven by God. Sin alienates us from God, and God's grace brings us to Him through forgiveness. Jesus' mission was not about solving human problems through politics, social programs, or crusades. Jesus' mission was about solving the sin problem that separates us from God. Jesus asked in Mark 8:36 "What good is it for someone to gain the whole world, yet forfeit their soul?" What do we benefit from solving the problems of this life, if we do not address the problems of the next?

The saying of Jesus in the present reading is about this problem. Jesus said: "*And when you stand praying, if you hold anything against anyone, forgive them, so that your Father in heaven may forgive you your sins.*" It would be easy to misunderstand Jesus' words here, and assume that he is simply making a logical statement: if you do not forgive, your Father in heaven will not forgive you. Sometimes we read this as if God's actions of grace to us are dependent on our actions of grace to others. If we do not forgive others, God will not forgive us. God is watching to see if we have forgiven others. If so, He will forgive us.

I think that this understanding misses Jesus' point completely. God's grace is of His own initiative, not ours. Grace that depends on our being righteous is not grace at all! Grace is just the opposite of this idea. Grace is God's mercy poured out on us when we are unrighteous. God is not waiting to see what we will do before He shows grace. He is not counting the sins we have not forgiven other people to see how many of our sins He can forgive.

So how should we understand Jesus' words here? This is what I think he meant: when you stand praying, be sure you are standing in grace. A life of grace both receives forgiveness, and bestows it on others. It is not a logical equation, but a heart condition. It's as if Jesus said: "when you pray, be sure you are a person who shows grace to others, so that you are really living in the grace God shows you."

If we are living in grace, then God's Holy Spirit is doing something in our lives. He is changing us to become more like Christ. God's desire is to make us holy. This is why Paul said in I Thessalonians 4:3 "It is God's will that you should be sanctified . . ." If we are God's people through faith in Jesus Christ, God is working out His will in our hearts, to make us holy. If we stand praying, and cannot show grace to those who have wronged us, we still don't understand grace. We don't have God's perspective about forgiveness. I believe this is what Jesus meant. When you stand praying, make sure you "get" grace—giving and receiving it.

Are there people you have not forgiven? Is there someone who has hurt you deeply, and you cannot forgive? Consider that you have hurt God with your sins, yet He forgives through faith in Jesus Christ. If God can forgive you for your sins against Him, how can you not forgive that person for his or her sins against you?

There is power in grace. God's grace can save you from your sins. Showing God's grace to those who have wronged you can release you from years of anger, resentment, and frustration, and restore God's joy and peace to your heart. The more you practice forgiveness, the better you understand God's grace in your life.

22

Render Unto Caesar
Mark 12:13–17

¹³ Later they sent some of the Pharisees and Herodians to Jesus to catch him in his words. ¹⁴ They came to him and said, "Teacher, we know that you are a man of integrity. You aren't swayed by others, because you pay no attention to who they are; but you teach the way of God in accordance with the truth. Is it right to pay the imperial tax to Caesar or not? ¹⁵ Should we pay or shouldn't we?"

But Jesus knew their hypocrisy. "Why are you trying to trap me?" he asked. "Bring me a denarius and let me look at it." ¹⁶ They brought the coin, and he asked them, "Whose image is this? And whose inscription?"

"Caesar's," they replied.

¹⁷ Then Jesus said to them, "Give back to Caesar what is Caesar's and to God what is God's."

And they were amazed at him.

THE CONFRONTATION WHICH ENDED in vs. 12 spilled over into a new confrontation, as those Jesus had rebuked sent other groups of people to trap him. This time, the Pharisees and the Herodians came to publically challenge Jesus. This is not the first alliance Mark has depicted between these groups. After Jesus ensnared the Pharisees in their own trap and healed a man with a withered hand, the Pharisees went and began conspiring with the Herodians about how they might destroy Jesus (Mark. 3:6). The Pharisees were interested in maintaining ritual purity through obedience to the Law of Moses and in retaining power over the religious life of Israel by enforcing obedience to the Law.

Mark seems to assume that his audience is familiar with the Herodians, and does not take pains to define them. These people may have been members of Herod's extended family or his court, or perhaps even Jews who saw Herod as a messianic figure.[1] They were "a rather heterogeneous group of influential aristocrats who were pro-Herod in sentiment."[2] These Jews were interested in maintaining the status quo in the governance of Judea. The family of Herod served as vassal kings under the authority of Caesar. The Herod bloodline was partially Jewish, and Herod the Great had funded renovations to the Temple. It may be that the Herodians feared that if the Herods were replaced with gentile vassal kings, the Jews would not be as well-treated as they were under the Herod family. It may also be that "Herodians" was a more informal term to describe those who supported Herod, rather than the name of a specific political party.

One group was religious, the other was secular, and their goals were very different. However, Jesus presented an obstacle to both the religious power of the Pharisees and the civil tranquility sought by the Herodians, so they aligned against him.

The Pharisees and Herodians began with sarcasm, masked as flattery, then followed immediately with a loaded question about paying taxes to Caesar. This was a public challenge to Jesus. If Jesus answered that people should pay taxes to Caesar (to the Roman government), then he would lose support among the Jewish people who hated the Romans and their oppressive taxation. If he answered that the Jews should not pay taxes to Rome, then

---

1. Rowley, "The Herodians in the Gospels", 14–27.
2. Bennett, "The Herodians of Mark's Gospel", 10.

he would be guilty of sedition, and the Herodians were present to witness against him in court.

Jesus saw clearly that this was a trap, and asked for a coin. When his challengers produced one, he examined it and asked whose inscription was on it. This question itself would probably be considered a challenge, because everyone knew whose inscription was on the coin. The question indicated to the Pharisees and Herodians that they had missed the point all along—that the answer to their question was stamped onto the coin they were holding. The image, of course, was that of Caesar.

Jesus had been challenged publically, had issued a counter-challenge in the form of a question, and now pronounced his verdict: "Render unto Caesar that which is Caesar's, and unto God that which is God's." There is no inherent conflict between civil and religious obedience, so long as one does not intrude upon the other. Jews of Jesus' day (and Christians of our own day) can honor God and submit to civil authority. As a result of his response, the Pharisees and Herodians were "amazed" at him. Clearly, these groups believed that one or the other of them would ensnare Jesus, based on how he answered the question. He has answered, however, in a way in which none could find fault.

Followers of Jesus Christ should be excellent citizens. Our belief that God uses civil government for the good of mankind (as in Romans 13) leads us to submit to authority, to obey the law, to pay our taxes, and to keep the peace. There is a point, however, at which obedience to God overrides obedience to the state. As long as the state remains within its proper boundaries and prescribes laws for the governing of society, there is no conflict, but when the state asserts authority over the conscience—telling citizens what to believe, how to worship, or requiring support for acts of immorality, for example—the Christ-follower peacefully refuses to acknowledge the authority of the state over the conscience, and maintains obedience to God. Thus we render unto Caesar that which is Caesar's, and unto God that which is God's.

Are your priorities in line? Have you ordered your life in a way such that God receives all that is due to Him? Are you living in obedience to the laws of the land? Do you live like a Pharisee, trusting in your own righteousness? Are you a Herodian, hoping that the right politician can solve your problems? Only a rightly ordered life, with every priority in its proper place, can honor God fully and bring you into a deeper relationship with Him.

23

Jesus Teaches the Greatest Commandment

Mark 12:28–31

[28] One of the teachers of the law came and heard them debating. Noticing that Jesus had given them a good answer, he asked him, "Of all the commandments, which is the most important?"

[29] "The most important one," answered Jesus, "is this: 'Hear, O Israel: The Lord our God, the Lord is one. [30] Love the Lord your God with all your heart and with all your soul and with all your mind and with all your strength.' [31] The second is this: 'Love your neighbor as yourself.' There is no commandment greater than these."

THE END OF MARK 11 and the beginning of Mark 12 describe three conflicts Jesus had with the religious authorities of his day. They challenged his authority (11:28), they tried to have him arrested for insurrection against Caesar (12:14–15), and they tried to trip him up with a tricky theological question (12:18–23). Each time, Jesus answered in such a way that his opponents were dumbfounded. Jesus met each challenge with a response that showed his wisdom.

A certain scribe had been watching these three challenges to Jesus, and had heard Jesus' response. After the dust had settled, he came to Jesus with a question—not a challenge, but a sincere question of his own. This scribe's question is relevant for our lives as well: "Of all the commandments, which is the most important?" In other words, where should we put our priorities if we want to please God? What matters most to God, and should matter most to us? Jesus gave this scribe a simple, straightforward answer, quoting the *Shema*. The *Shema* is found in Deuteronomy 6:4–9, and was recited daily by Jews. It is called the *Shema* after the first word in the text: the Hebrew word *shema* means "hear". The *Shema* says:

> Hear, O Israel: The Lord our God, the Lord is one. Love the Lord your God with all your heart and with all your soul and with all your strength. These commandments that I give you today are to be on your hearts. Impress them on your children. Talk about them when you sit at home and when you walk along the road, when you lie down and when you get up. Tie them as symbols on your hands and bind them on your foreheads. Write them on the doorframes of your houses and on your gates.

The most important commandment is to love God with all one's being: heart, soul, and strength. That is, we should love God with our emotions, our motivations, and our actions. God's greatest priority for us is that we love Him.

Jesus added another commandment, the second greatest—to love one's neighbor as oneself. Jesus here quoted Leviticus 19:18, which says *"Do not seek revenge or bear a grudge against anyone among your people, but love your neighbor as yourself. I am the Lord."*

The two greatest commandments are to love God and to love other people. What makes these two commandments greater than all the others? Perhaps Matthew gives us a clue in his gospel. When Matthew recorded these words of Jesus, he added some words that Mark did not: "All the Law and the Prophets hang on these two commandments" (Matthew 22:40).

The Law was written to tell the Jews how to relate to God and to other people. By the time of Jesus, the Jews had identified over

Jesus Teaches the Greatest Commandment

600 individual commandments in the Law of Moses. Some Jews, like the Pharisees, were convinced that if they could keep all these rules, for all their lives, they would be right with God.

Think about what a burden this would be! Can you imagine if your relationship with God were based on your ability to memorize over 600 rules and never break them throughout your lifetime? Do you think that you could ever be right with God under these circumstances?

The prophets of the Old Testament were sent by God to get His people back on track. When the Jews would exploit the poor, or worship idols, or fall into some other sin, God would send a prophet to speak His word to them, to remind them that they are His people, and to urge them to repent. The Old Testament demonstrates a perpetual cycle of the Israelites falling away, receiving God's judgment, and repenting of their sins, just to fall away again. God sent prophets to call His people back to Himself.

Jesus said that the command to love God and love our neighbor encompasses all the Law and the prophets. What he meant is that if we will love God and love our neighbor, we do not need to worry about the 600-something commandments in the Law, and we will not need prophets to call us back to God. Loving God first and loving others as ourselves means that we will not live a life of sin against God or others. If God is our first priority, and our neighbors are a close second, then our actions, motivations, and emotions will fall into line.

Humans are created with a capacity to love that is unmatched in all of creation. Animals may feel a sense of affection or devotion, but they can never love like we can. Animals operate out of instinct, but we can choose to act out of love. Quite simply, we were made to love. It is how God has designed us.

God's desire that we love Him is the whole point of Jesus Christ's birth! It's hard for us to love *ideas*. Our hearts are oriented toward loving *people*. So God sent His Son, Jesus Christ, as a man, as a real person. To love God is to love Jesus Christ, and a love for Jesus motivates us to love others.

If our hearts are right, our minds and actions will follow. What is the greatest thing you can do with your life? Love God, and love others. Are you demonstrating your love for God by loving those whom He loves? Is your love expressed in your words and actions?

24

Jesus Will Return for his Elect
Mark 13:24–27

²⁴ "But in those days, following that distress,
 "'the sun will be darkened, and the moon will not give its light;
²⁵ the stars will fall from the sky, and the heavenly bodies will be shaken.'
 ²⁶ "At that time people will see the Son of Man coming in clouds with great power and glory. ²⁷ And he will send his angels and gather his elect from the four winds, from the ends of the earth to the ends of the heavens.

MANKIND HAS ALWAYS BEEN fascinated with the idea of the end of time. We have always had the idea that history is leading up to something, that there is a cosmic purpose toward which all of life is moving. The ancient Jews believed in the "day of the Lord", when God would come to earth to set all things right. God would punish the wicked and bless the righteous. Here is an example of Old Testament teachings about the day of the Lord:

> "Blow the trumpet in Zion; sound the alarm on my holy hill. Let all who live in the land tremble, for the day of the Lord is coming. It is close at hand—a day of darkness and gloom, a day of clouds and blackness. Like dawn

spreading across the mountains a large and mighty army comes, such as never was in ancient times nor ever will be in ages to come.

Joel 2:1–2

Jesus also taught about a final, cosmic day of the Lord. He said that his return would be the day of the Lord predicted by the prophets of old. Many of the Jews imagined that the Messiah would come on the day of the Lord, but they did not understand that first he would be born of a virgin, live, teach, and heal, then die and rise again. They understood the end of the Messiah's ministry, but not the beginning. Throughout Mark's gospel, we have seen the ministry of Jesus the Messiah unfold. Now he is teaching about a ministry yet to come—his ministry of returning for his people.

Many people have attempted to construct timelines, theologies, and biblical studies to help understand biblical teachings about the return of Christ. It is a complex issue, and is made more difficult by the fact that many of the prophecies about the return of Christ, such as in Daniel and Revelation, are expressed in apocalyptic imagery that is hard to interpret.

Many Christians struggle to understand the relationship between events surrounding the end times. Will Jesus come before, during, or after the tribulation described in Revelation? Will there be a rapture of the church? What will be the signs of his coming? These are important theological questions, but I don't think they are primary ones. In other words, there are more important things for Christians to focus on than figuring out God's plan for the end of time. In fact, in our next reflection we will see that Jesus said we can't know when he will return.

I think that the most important aspect of this passage for us is the fact that Jesus will return for his elect. On that day—whenever it is—Jesus will come for his own, and will gather them to himself. We don't have to know exactly when that will be to take great comfort from this fact. No matter how bad things get in this world, all of history is moving toward the day when God will set all things right. In his 1967 speech to the Southern Christian Leadership Conference, Dr. Martin Luther King, Jr. said "The arc of the moral

Jesus Will Return for His Elect

universe is long, but it bends toward justice." The universe indeed bends toward justice because it is guided by the eternal purpose of God, expressed in Jesus Christ.

The apostle Paul would later express the hope and joy of Christ's return like this in I Thessalonians 4:16–18:

For the Lord himself will come down from heaven, with a loud command, with the voice of the archangel and with the trumpet call of God, and the dead in Christ will rise first. After that, we who are still alive and are left will be caught up together with them in the clouds to meet the Lord in the air. And so we will be with the Lord forever. Therefore encourage one another with these words.

The great comfort of the gospel of Jesus Christ is that there is more to this life than this life. All of history—and your life as well—are moving toward God's final revelation of Himself in justice. Jesus came to show us God's love and grace. Are you living in the grace of God? Have you trusted Jesus Christ for the forgiveness of your sins? When Jesus returns, is he coming for you?

25

No One Knows the Hour

Mark 13:32-37

³² "But about that day or hour no one knows, not even the angels in heaven, nor the Son, but only the Father. ³³ Be on guard! Be alert! You do not know when that time will come. ³⁴ It's like a man going away: He leaves his house and puts his servants in charge, each with their assigned task, and tells the one at the door to keep watch.

³⁵ "Therefore keep watch because you do not know when the owner of the house will come back—whether in the evening, or at midnight, or when the rooster crows, or at dawn. ³⁶ If he comes suddenly, do not let him find you sleeping. ³⁷ What I say to you, I say to everyone: 'Watch!'"

PREVIOUSLY, WE DISCUSSED JESUS' prediction that he would one day return for his elect. Ever since Jesus spoke those words, people have been trying to figure out when he would return. For two thousand years, Christians have been fascinated (sometimes more than at other times) with the return of Jesus. In our own day, Christian bookstores are packed with books about the end times. Popular movies depict some peoples' interpretation of how the return of

Christ will take place. There are numerous conferences on the end times held through the United States every year.

Jesus anticipated this obsession with figuring out his return. Immediately after predicting his return, Jesus told this parable about a man who sent on a journey. This was not just any man, but a wealthy, powerful man. Before he left on his journey, he assigned tasks to his servants for the upkeep of the house. He posted a doorman at the door to keep watch. A "great house" in the Middle East would have a large wall around it, and access would be granted only by going through the main gate. The doorman would watch for the arrival of the master, and keep unauthorized visitors out of the master's house. In this parable, the master might return any time, so the servants must keep watch as they performed their assigned duties.

Jesus repeated the moral of his story so that we might not miss it: "*What I say to you, I say to everyone: 'Watch'!*" Clearly, the message Jesus wanted us to get from his parable was to watch and to work.

Now, this text comes in the middle of a larger passage in which Jesus discussed two different events which were still in the future. One is the fall of Jerusalem and the destruction of the Temple, which occurred in the year 70 AD. The other is Jesus' return at the end of the age. He intertwined his teaching on each of these events, so much so that we are left without clarity on which events are referenced in some parts of this passage. This has led to confusion about how to interpret Jesus' references to his return. We can read what Jesus said, but we are still not quite sure what he meant.

I think this was Jesus' purpose all along. He knew that if we had enough clues to figure out the end times, we would be fixated on it. Indeed, even with what we do know, many Christians today place a very high priority—sometimes too high a priority—on Jesus' return. You may ask, what is wrong with this?

I don't think Jesus' desire is that his people sit around calendars and brood over obscure texts, or that they obsess over relating current events to the fulfillment of biblical prophecy. Certainly, we should care about Jesus' return. The book of Revelation even promises an eternal reward to those who love and anticipate Jesus' return. In the military there is a term for those soldiers whose retirement is drawing near: short-timers. It is generally assumed (whether it is true or not) that short-timers will not give their full effort to their work, because they know that they will soon be discharged. It is assumed that they are not in it for the long haul. Jesus did not want us to live as short-timers, detached from this world. He wanted us to live, work, pray, and love each other fully in our lives here and now, with an eye out for the return of our master.

This is why in this parable, the master assigned tasks to every servant. He warns them *"If he comes suddenly, do not let him find you sleeping."* God is more glorified, and we are more fulfilled in our lives, when our focus is on living holy, productive lives of ministry, faithfulness, and obedience than when our priority is on solving riddles of biblical prophecy.

In Jesus' parable, the master assigned his servants two responsibilities—to work and to watch. Let's not get so busy watching that we neglect the work God has given us to do. One day, Jesus will return. Let him find us faithful in our Father's business!

26

Calculation vs. Devotion
Mark 14:3–9

³ While he was in Bethany, reclining at the table in the home of Simon the Leper, a woman came with an alabaster jar of very expensive perfume, made of pure nard. She broke the jar and poured the perfume on his head.

⁴ Some of those present were saying indignantly to one another, "Why this waste of perfume? ⁵ It could have been sold for more than a year's wages and the money given to the poor." And they rebuked her harshly.

⁶ "Leave her alone," said Jesus. "Why are you bothering her? She has done a beautiful thing to me. ⁷ The poor you will always have with you, and you can help them any time you want. But you will not always have me. ⁸ She did what she could. She poured perfume on my body beforehand to prepare for my burial. ⁹ Truly I tell you, wherever the gospel is preached throughout the world, what she has done will also be told, in memory of her."

IN THIS PASSAGE JESUS has returned from Jerusalem to the village of Bethany. Mark situates him in the home of Simon the Leper.

The fact that Simon is in his own home indicates that he is not currently a leper, as lepers were not permitted to mingle with others due to the highly contagious nature of their disease. The gospels do not provide an account of Jesus' healing of Simon, though it may be assumed that perhaps Jesus has healed Simon of his leprosy, which would account for both Simon's acceptance in society, and Jesus' presence in his house.

In this story, a woman came into Simon's home and anointed Jesus' head with a bottle of expensive perfume. She broke the vial containing the perfume, and poured it out for Jesus. Her sacrifice was a complete offering, with nothing held back. Such a sacrifice was rare indeed. An expensive bottle of perfume may have been this woman's dowry, or perhaps an inheritance. It would not have been a luxury item she kept in her bathroom cabinet and enjoyed herself. It would have been an investment—an item of value she kept for her own financial security.

Some people, probably disciples of Jesus, were taken aback at the costly offering the woman brought. The perfume could have been sold and given to the poor. They were right, of course—there were more practical uses for it than anointing Jesus. However, this offering was hers to give, and she gave it to Christ as she saw fit. The woman was expressing her devotion to Jesus, while the disciples were engaged in calculation about God's work.

Jesus rebuked those who scolded the woman. There would be plenty of opportunities to minister to the poor, Jesus said, and the disciples would be expected to be faithful in these opportunities. However, Jesus was going to the cross, and she had anointed him for his burial. There is a time for ministry to others, and there is a time for devotion to Christ. Jesus predicted—quite correctly—that an account of this woman's sacrifice would be preserved and repeated wherever the gospel is preached.

This really gets to the heart of the gospel. Christians believe that Jesus is the incarnation of God—that the eternal Son of God became a man, born of a virgin, who grew, lived, laughed, worked, taught, healed, died, and rose again. Jesus is not a cause to work for, an idea to accept, an identity to take on, or a mission

Calculation vs. Devotion

to complete. He is a person—God and man in one—to love. He is a friend to sinners, a faithful brother in the Kingdom of God. He did not come simply to put people to work. He has angels who can do his work, and do it much better than we can! He came to give and receive God's love. He came to show God's love and call us to love him in return.

In this moment, the woman loved Jesus. His suffering and death were close, so she comforted him with a beautiful gesture of devotion. The disciples were so focused on the ministry Jesus had shown them that he became simply a figurehead for their work. They did not, in this moment, see Jesus as a man, but only as a mission.

Let us be careful that we do not allow ourselves to become so absorbed in the mission of Jesus that we do not see him as he is: God with us, a friend, savior, the love of God in human form. Loving God is a matter of devotion, not calculation, and it does not always make sense to those around us.

27

Jesus Institutes a New Covenant
Mark 14:22-25

²² While they were eating, Jesus took bread, and when he had given thanks, he broke it and gave it to his disciples, saying, "Take it; this is my body."
²³ Then he took a cup, and when he had given thanks, he gave it to them, and they all drank from it.
²⁴ "This is my blood of the covenant, which is poured out for many," he said to them. ²⁵ "Truly I tell you, I will not drink again from the fruit of the vine until that day when I drink it new in the kingdom of God."

PERHAPS NO CHRISTIAN RITUAL has held more meaning throughout the history of the church than the one Jesus instituted on this night. Christians have called it by different names—the eucharist, the Lord's Supper, communion—and have differed in their theological understanding of some aspects of its meaning, but followers of Jesus Christ everywhere have agreed that eating the bread and drinking the wine is an incredibly profound and meaningful experience.

The setting was not unusual for devout Jewish men. They had gathered in an upper room to celebrate the Passover. The Passover was an annual Jewish feast which commemorated God's deliverance of Israel from slavery in Egypt so many years before. God sent Moses to liberate His people from the hand of Pharaoh, but Pharaoh was hard-hearted, and refused to let them go. God sent plagues on Egypt to trouble them into releasing the Israelites, one worse than the next, but each time, Pharaoh refused. Nine plagues came and went. Finally, the tenth and final plague would be visited on Egypt. This plague would break the back of the Egyptians, and prove so devastating that they would release the nation of Israel to return to the land God had promised to Abraham.

What was this tenth plague? The angel of death would pass through Egypt, killing the first-born of every household. From the highest to the lowest, every home would feel death's icy grasp that night. In the morning, cries of mourning would be heard from Cairo to Luxor. It was a terrible judgment, and demonstrates God's great desire to save His people. God does not take life lightly, and had tried nine times before to persuade Egypt to let His people go. God had a purpose to fulfill through Israel; He had a promise to keep.

Moses warned the people of Israel that the angel of death was coming. They were to sacrifice a lamb and smear its blood over their doorposts. Poor families could join together and share a lamb, but no matter what, every Jewish home must have the blood of the lamb on their door posts. Then, when the angel of death came through Egypt, he would pass over these homes, sparing the first born. Thus, the feast of Passover celebrates God's "passing over" His people in judgment. You can read about this in Exodus 11 and 12.

Now Jesus and his friends have gathered to celebrate God's deliverance of Israel. Little did the Jews understand what Jesus would reveal to them in the next few days! The symbolism of Passover could not be a stronger foretaste of what God would do for His people through Jesus Christ. The blood of the lamb had saved the Jews from the judgment of God. Now, the blood of the Lamb would save the world!

Jesus took the main elements of the meal, the bread and wine, and infused new meaning into them. The bread, which the ancient Jews had eaten in haste, ready to leave Egypt at a moment's notice, had been baked without yeast. As a result, it was more like a large cracker than the soft, chewy bread they usually ate. When eating the Passover feast, they would break off pieces. As Jesus snapped off a piece, he told his friends that the bread represented his own body, which would be broken for them. Jesus clearly understood that his ministry would lead him to the cross, and that his death on the cross would save his people.

Jesus referred to the wine as the "blood of the covenant". The Old Testament covenant with God was sealed with blood. Animal sacrifices were required to atone for the sins of the nation of Israel, and for individual people. The author of Hebrews, looking back on the sacrificial system of the Old Testament, wrote "the law requires that nearly everything be cleansed with blood, and without the shedding of blood there is no forgiveness." (Hebrews 9:22). On the cross the next day, Jesus would be the sacrificial Lamb of God, shedding his blood for our salvation.

One of Jesus' friends who was at this meal, and then later stood with Jesus a while at the cross, was John. John would later write: "the blood of Jesus, his Son, purifies us from all sin." (I John 1:7). This Passover meal with Jesus set the stage for a new ritual, which is still observed among Jesus' followers today. Just as the Jews gathered to celebrate God's deliverance of Israel by reenacting that terrible night of judgment in the Passover meal, Christians join together in remembering the suffering and death of Jesus on the cross. When John the Baptist first saw Jesus, he said to those gathered around him "Look, the Lamb of God, who takes away the sin of the world!" (John 1:29). When Jesus' followers today celebrate the Lord's Supper, they remember that Jesus died for their sins, so they could be saved.

Take some time today to reflect on Jesus' suffering and death for your sins. Have you fully grasped the significance of Jesus' broken body and shed blood? What does it mean to you?

28

Jesus, King of the Jews
Mark 15:1–5

Very early in the morning, the chief priests, with the elders, the teachers of the law and the whole Sanhedrin, made their plans. So they bound Jesus, led him away and handed him over to Pilate.
² "Are you the king of the Jews?" asked Pilate.
"You have said so," Jesus replied.
³ The chief priests accused him of many things. ⁴ So again Pilate asked him, "Aren't you going to answer? See how many things they are accusing you of."
⁵ But Jesus still made no reply, and Pilate was amazed.

THE RELIGIOUS LEADERS WANTED to get Jesus' trial over quickly, before the crowds knew what was going on. Early in the morning, having had Jesus in trials all night, they bound Jesus and brought him to Pilate. Pontius Pilate was the Roman prefect of Judea, a regional governor representing Caesar. He was the administrator of Roman law. Jews were permitted to practice their religion freely, and to impose religious sanctions for religious violations, but were not permitted to execute criminals. This right was held by Rome, so the Jewish religious leaders would need for Pilate to order Jesus' execution. Pilate would not execute Jesus for his disagreements with the religious leaders, so they would need criminal charges to bring before him. They needed a charge that would carry the death penalty: treason.

The Jews were under the authority of the emperor, Caesar, and any claim to kingship would be seen as an attempt to rally the Jews for rebellion against Rome. Jesus affirmed the charge—"it is as you say". Perhaps there is an element of sarcasm here. Pilate clearly did not take the charges seriously. In Mark and the other gospels, he does not treat Jesus like a rebel or insurrectionist. Perhaps Pilate has expressed the charges with a tone and body language that indicate doubt or contempt for these charges, and Jesus affirmed, as if to say "these charges are what you think they are". Nevertheless, Jesus also spoke the truth here. He was the King of the Jews, the long-awaited Messiah who will sit on the throne of David forever.

The chief priests took this cue to pile accusations on Jesus. Perhaps they sensed that Pilate did not take them seriously, so they felt compelled to argue their accusations more vehemently. Pilate was accustomed to litigating arguments. He frequently saw accused criminals and their accusers debate vigorously, each trying to sway him toward their side and win their case. Jesus made no such attempt, but kept silent. Pilate was amazed at his demeanor. This is particularly significant when we consider that Jesus' life was at stake. We would expect any man to fight for his life, especially an innocent man. But Jesus made no attempt to save himself.

Why didn't Jesus try to save himself? Because he was saving you and me. The cross was the purpose for Jesus' birth, his life, his teachings. Everything Jesus did was to lead up to his death on the cross. Remember, the greatest human problem is sin, and our greatest need is someone to save us from our sin. Jesus is that Savior. Could he have talked his way out of the cross? Of course! Jesus could have avoided the suffering and shame of the cross, but that was not his purpose. Luke tells us that as the time drew near for his crucifixion, "Jesus resolutely set out for Jerusalem." (Luke 9:51).

Matthew records Jesus' arrest in the garden. One of Jesus' disciples (John tells us that it was Peter) drew his sword to fight. Jesus told him to put the sword away. Jesus said: "Do you think I cannot call on my Father, and he will at once put at my disposal more than twelve legions of angels? But how then would the Scriptures be fulfilled that say it must happen in this way?" (Matthew 26:53–54).

Jesus' greatest concern was not for his safety, or his comfort, or his reputation. He did not come to achieve any of these things.

Charles Sell expressed the mission of Jesus clearly in his book *Unfinished Business*:

If our greatest need had been information, God would have sent us an educator. If our greatest need had been technology, God would have sent us a scientist. If our greatest need had been money, God would have sent us an economist. If our greatest need had been pleasure, God would have sent us an entertainer. But our greatest need was forgiveness, so God sent us a Savior.[1]

That's why Jesus did not speak up for himself. He did not come to live, but to die for your sins and mine. He did not come to vindicate himself, but to justify sinners. We have often heard that actions speak louder than words, and in no case is this more true and powerful than in Jesus' death on the cross.

---

1. Sell, *Unfinished Business*, 121–122.

29

Jesus Forsaken
Mark 15:33–34

³³ At noon, darkness came over the whole land until three in the afternoon. ³⁴ And at three in the afternoon Jesus cried out in a loud voice, "Eloi, Eloi, lema sabachthani?" (which means "My God, my God, why have you forsaken me?").

ALL THROUGH HIS GOSPEL, Mark has situated Jesus in time and space. He has depicted Jesus on the sea, on the road, on the mountain, in Judea, in Galilee. He has given his readers a temporal understanding of Jesus through his keyword "immediately", as one event flows into another. Now, Mark amplifies his focus on time, because the events of Jesus' life have come to a head. If this were a movie, the camera would zoom in on Jesus, time would slow down, and the ominous orchestral music would begin. Jesus is no longer walking and laughing in the sunshine by the shores of Galilee. He is not surrounded by friends. He is dying, naked and alone under a black sky.

For three hours Jesus hung in darkness, nailed to two rough-hewn wooden beams, suffering from the scourging he received the night before. For three hours the heavens ceased to glow as the Son of God was dying for sins of mankind.

Jesus cried out in his native Aramaic: "My God, my God, why have You forsaken me?" Surely, this was a God-forsaken moment of darkness and death. But Jesus' cry is not merely shout of anguish, despair, and raging against his coming death. Like everything else Jesus did, these words are loaded with meaning. Jesus was quoting Psalm 22, which begins with the question "My God, my God, why have You forsaken me?" Throughout the psalm, David cries out to the Lord that he is suffering, that enemies have surrounded him, that friends have forsaken him, and that the whole world witnesses his shame. This psalm is a powerful prediction of the suffering and death of Jesus on the cross. Read verses 16–18: "Dogs surround me, a pack of villains encircles me; they pierce my hands and my feet. All my bones are on display; people stare and gloat over me. They divide my clothes among them and cast lots for my garment." The gospels describe the death of Jesus in exactly these terms.

When Jesus cried out that God had forsaken him, he was directing our attention to this psalm. Read psalm 22 and see for yourself the suffering and despair of the Messiah. He would die alone, God-forsaken, surrounded by gentile enemies. Everything this psalm predicted was fulfilled in Jesus' suffering and death on the cross.

Yet the psalm does not end with suffering and death. Verse 24 says that God has indeed heard the psalmist's cries for help. He has listened to the afflicted one. This moment is not God-forsaken, but God-ordained. Revelation 13:8 calls Jesus "the Lamb who was slain from the creation of the world." From the earliest beginnings, this was always the plan. God was always going to save His people from their sins through the sacrificial death of Jesus Christ, His Son, on the cross. Everything that God had done to reveal Himself to humanity—the Law, the prophets, the Temple, everything—pointed to this very moment. As Jesus cried out to God, it was not only because he was in anguish, but because he wanted to show us the significance of this anguish. His suffering and death were not tragic or meaningless. In his suffering was victory, and in his death was triumph.

Look at how psalm 22 ends. After the suffering of the afflicted one, "All the ends of the earth will remember and turn to the Lord, and all the families of the nations will bow down before him, for dominion belongs to the Lord and he rules over the nations" (Psalm 22:27–28). Jesus' suffering and death would lead the nations of the earth to give praise to God. All the ends of the earth would turn to the Lord because of Jesus' death. And that is exactly what has happened. An obscure carpenter from Galilee has captured the hearts of billions of people over a period of two thousand years! He never wrote a book, ruled a kingdom, raised an army, or traveled farther than he could walk, but he has followers from all over the world. Who else but God could do this?

Psalm 22 goes on to say: "Posterity will serve him; future generations will be told about the Lord. They will proclaim his righteousness, declaring to a people yet unborn: He has done it!"

What has he done? He has saved his people from their sins! In John 19:30 Jesus said simply: "It is finished". Then he died. On the cross, Jesus echoed the finality of the last words of Psalm 22. "He has done it!" "It is finished." God's great work of saving His people has been accomplished in Jesus Christ.

Jesus died for your sins, and for the sins of the world. Have you accepted his sacrifice on your behalf? Have you surrendered yourself to follow him? Is his work finished in your heart? Jesus' death demands a verdict from each of us. He has laid down his life in suffering and shame, and we cannot simply look away as if he has not. The stakes are high with Jesus—all or nothing. Where do you stand?

30

And Peter
Mark 16:6–7

⁶ "Don't be alarmed," he said. "You are looking for Jesus the Nazarene, who was crucified. He has risen! He is not here. See the place where they laid him. ⁷ But go, tell his disciples and Peter, 'He is going ahead of you into Galilee. There you will see him, just as he told you.'"

TWO DAYS HAVE PASSED since Jesus' death on the cross. We pick up here on the morning of the third day. Three courageous women have come to the tomb to properly anoint Jesus' body for burial. They have come to render one final act of love and devotion to Jesus Christ, the Son of God. Instead of a bloody corpse, a body executed by the Romans and hastily buried in the waning light of a Friday night, they find on this Sunday morning a young man, sitting in a white robe. Mark does not say it, but this is an angel, a messenger sent from God.

The angel tells the women not to be alarmed, though he has alarming news: Jesus is not here. In fact, he is not even dead. Not anymore. You can see where they laid him—blood stains on a linen sheet—but there is no body to anoint. Jesus Christ is alive and well!

There is more to the angel's message. Just as the women are beginning to grasp what is happening, they are commissioned to deliver a message: Jesus has returned to Galilee. For the disciples, Galilee was home. Their own homes, surrounded by their own families and familiar neighbors. Galilee was where they first met Jesus, and he called them to follow him. Jerusalem was a chaotic, unfamiliar urban jungle, but in Galilee, green fields and rolling hills spread for miles under a vast blue sky. Jesus was alive, and was in Galilee!

Notice, though, the audience for this message: "But go, tell his disciples and Peter". Jesus had many disciples, but Peter was singled out for special mention. God, speaking through the angel, wanted to make sure that Peter was included in the news of the resurrection, and was invited to Galilee to see Jesus again. Why Peter?

I think it is because Peter had denied Jesus three times, just as Jesus predicted that he would. Mark 14:66–72 records Peter's three denials of Jesus. Peter could not have denied Jesus any more strongly than he did. He swore an oath and called down curses on himself if he was lying: "I don't know this man." As Jesus was being tried and beaten, Peter was denying that he even knew Jesus.

Yet now, three days later, the angel's message includes Peter by name. The women might overlook Peter as they told the disciples the news of Jesus' resurrection, because Peter had opted out. Peter was no longer a disciple, right? Peter had been tested and had failed. He had his chance, and he blew it.

Think about this: Peter was not mentioned by name because of his great courage and devotion, but because of his failure. John had stood at the very foot of Jesus' cross, and had agreed to watch over Jesus' mother as his own (John 19:26), but he is not mentioned. The other disciples stood and watched at a distance, but none of them are called by name to Galilee. Very early in his ministry, in Mark 2:17, Jesus said that he had not come to call the righteous, but to call sinners. Peter had sinned, and now Jesus was calling him back home. What a beautiful picture of grace! Peter had sworn three times that he did not know Jesus. God's response was "I know you, Peter. Come home and see me again." Later, Jesus and Peter would sit and eat together on the shore of the Sea of Galilee. Peter would confess his love for Jesus, and Jesus would commission him to feed the flock of God. From that moment on, Peter would live for Jesus all his days. About thirty years later, Peter would lay down his life for the name of Jesus Christ. But it all started right here, when God called Peter by name.

God made the resurrection of Jesus personal for Peter. He makes it personal for you, too. Jesus did not simply die and rise again. He died for *your* sins, and rose again for *your* victory. Jesus' death was intensely personal, and his call to come to him is no less personal. Because of the resurrection, Jesus can call sinners to come to him. He has gone before us, and waits for us to follow.

Jesus came to call sinners. Are you a sinner? Of course you are—we are all sinners. Peter went so far in his sin as to curse and swear he did not know Jesus, but still Jesus called him. God's grace is so strong that he wanted to make sure Peter knew that no matter what he had done, Jesus was waiting for him. The same applies to you—no matter what your sin, or how long you have been mired in it, God's grace calls to you. The Bible says in Romans 10:9-13:

> If you declare with your mouth, "Jesus is Lord," and believe in your heart that God raised him from the dead, you will be saved. For it is with your heart that you believe and are justified, and it is with your mouth that you profess your faith and are saved. As Scripture says, "Anyone who believes in him will never be put to shame." For there is no difference between Jew and Gentile—the same Lord is Lord of all and richly blesses all who call on him, for, "Everyone who calls on the name of the Lord will be saved."

Will you call on the name of the Lord? Will you trust him to save you? Will you believe and confess that Jesus is Lord, and that God has raised him from the dead? You have spent a month reflecting on Jesus in the Gospel of Mark. What is your verdict?

Call on him today.

31

Jesus' Disciples Continue His Work
Mark 16:19-20

[19] After the Lord Jesus had spoken to them, he was taken up into heaven and he sat at the right hand of God. [20] Then the disciples went out and preached everywhere, and the Lord worked with them and confirmed his word by the signs that accompanied it.

MARK BEGAN BY WRITING about the "beginning of the gospel of Jesus Christ, the Son of God." Now he comes to the end of Jesus' earthly ministry, which culminated in his ascension into heaven. Luke describes Jesus' ascension in more detail in Acts 1, but Mark, in his characteristic style, simply states that Jesus was "taken up into heaven and sat at the right hand of God." Let's notice three important things in these verses that are still occurring today.

The first is that Jesus sat at the right hand of God. Theologians call this aspect of Jesus' ministry his "session". Sitting at the right hand of God represents a number of significant things. The first is his acceptance by the Father. Who but "Jesus Christ the Son of God" has a place reserved for him at the right hand of God? This seat of honor is for the Son, in whom God has twice expressed in Mark that He is well pleased. Second, it indicates the completion of Jesus' redemptive work. He sits down because his work is finished. What he began with his incarnation and birth, he has completed with his death and resurrection. Third, Jesus' session at the right hand of God signals the start of a new ministry. Paul explains in Romans 8:34 that Jesus has been raised from the dead, has ascended into heaven, and sits at the right hand of God, making intercession for us. Jesus sits as a high priest, interceding on our behalf to the Father. Jesus has finished his work, is approved by the Father, and intercedes for us.

Second, notice the response of the disciples. They "went out and preached everywhere." Jesus' ascension into heaven was the end of his earthly ministry, but their ministries were just beginning. They lived in expectation of Jesus' return, and while they waited, they were faithful to preach the gospel. Tradition tells us that these men scattered across the known world, and almost all of them laid down their lives for their faith. Peter was crucified upside down in Rome, James the son of Zebedee was executed by Herod, and Thomas ended his ministry preaching in India. Andrew preached in Turkey and even traveled to the then-savage people of modern-day Russia. Phillip's ministry took him to North Africa, while Matthew is said to have preached in Persia and Ethiopia. Bartholomew took the gospel to Armenia and southern Arabia. James the son of Alpheus laid down his life preaching in Syria. Simon the zealot went to the warrior people of Persia and preached the gospel. After refusing to worship the sun god, he was put to death. Only John died a natural death, but he served a lengthy prison sentence in exile on the island of Patmos.

From the days of the apostles to our very own time, the gospel marches on. Faithful Christ-followers continue to preach the gospel in large and small ways—to crowds of thousands and one-on-one with friends. What about you? Are you a disciple, preaching the gospel?

Third, see that "the Lord worked with them and confirmed his word". When Jesus sent his disciples out to preach the gospel, he filled them with power, boldness, and wisdom to preach in such a way that the truth of their words would be confirmed. In the book of Acts, we see many miracles performed by the disciples to prove that they were indeed preaching the message of God. Today, these kinds of miracles are very uncommon, because the truth of the gospel has been established. God's power is no less active, however, in the lives of believers who take seriously His call to share the gospel of Jesus Christ. Jesus said in Acts 1:8 "you shall receive power when the Holy Spirit has come upon you, and you shall be my witnesses . . ." The same power that animated these early disciples to take the gospel throughout the world animates followers of Jesus Christ today. He still sits at the right hand of the Father, his disciples still preach the gospel everywhere, and the Lord still helps them.

What about you? If you are a follower of Jesus, are you preaching the gospel throughout your world? Are you telling the story of Jesus to those who need to hear it? If you are not, will you start today? Will you spend your life following Jesus?

Bibliography

Bennett, W. T. "The Herodians of Mark's Gospel." *Novum Testamentum* 17 1 (1975), 10.

Dark, K. *Archaeological Evidence for a Previously Unrecognised Roman Town Near the Sea of Galilee.* In Palestine Exploration Quarterly 145 3 (2013) 196.

Davis, John D. *Davis Dictionary of the Bible, Fourth Revised Edition.* Nashville: Broadman, 1972.

Lewis, C. S. *Mere Christianity.* New York: Touchstone, 1996.

Peterson, Eugene. "Saint Mark: The Basic Text for Christian Spirituality." *Crux* 29 4 (1993).

Rowley, H. H. "The Herodians in the Gospels." In *Journal of Theological Studies* XLI (1940) 14–27.

Sell, Charles. *Unfinished Business.* Eugene, OR: Multnomah, 1989.

www.ingramcontent.com/pod-product-compliance
Lightning Source LLC
Chambersburg PA
CBHW070932160426
43193CB00011B/1662